THE MELON
CAPITAL OF
THE WORLD

A Memoir

Blake Allmendinger

University of Nebraska Press
Lincoln and London

Library of Congress
Cataloging-in-Publication Data
Allmendinger, Blake.
The melon capital of the world: a
memoir / Blake Allmendinger.
pages   cm
ISBN 978-0-8032-5540-1 (cloth: alk. paper)
ISBN 978-0-8032-5665-1 (epub)
ISBN 978-0-8032-5666-8 (mobi)
ISBN 978-0-8032-5664-4 (pdf)
1. Rocky Ford (Colo.) — Biography.
2. Adult children of divorced
parents — United States — Biography.
3. Baby boom generation — United
States — Biography. 4. Rocky
Ford (Colo.) — Social life and
customs — Anecdotes. I. Title.
F784.R84A55 2014
978.8'95 — dc23   2014021537

Set in Bulmer by Lindsey Auten.
Designed by N. Putens.

For my father

Contents

Illustrations

THE MELON

CAPITAL OF

THE WORLD

Fig. 1. Although it appears Mom won the contest in 1958, she was actually first runner-up. Author's collection.

CHAPTER ONE

The Melon Capital of the World

My mother entered a beauty pageant when she was a sopho-more in college. Knowing the winner would be chosen by members of the audience, she invited my father and his fra-ternity buddies. They stopped at a bar on the night of the contest, and when they arrived at Mom's sorority, the winner had already been crowned.

Mom lost by a single vote.

The woman who beat her advanced in the competition and defeated other campus sorority queens for the title of Miss Colorado A&M. She lost the Miss Colorado pageant to a rival from another state university. The winner, Marilyn Van Derbur, was ultimately awarded the national crown.

For the rest of her life Mom blamed Dad for spoiling her chance to become Miss America.

Later in her autobiography Van Derbur admitted her father had molested her. A reporter announced the news on TV. My mother picked up the clicker and said with satisfaction as the screen faded to black, "Everything evens out in the end."

Mom's dream of stardom was thwarted by circumstances beyond her control. Her only consolation was taking pleasure in the misfortunes of others. My mother was raised in a farming community on the plains of southeastern Colorado. She was president of her 4-H club, a trick rider, the lead twirler with the marching band, valedictorian of her high school class, and the youngest contestant ever to win the title of Miss Rocky Ford.

Mom turned down the opportunity to go to Cornell University when her father was diagnosed with terminal lung cancer. She enrolled at Colorado A&M and came home on weekends to help nurse her father until he died. My grandfather expressed concerns about the family's finances in a letter he wrote to my mother. "Dear Rosie How are you I am Sick a Bed . . . . Car Business Pretty Slow can't Make any Money any more guess I will Take Old Age Pension and Retire," he joked. He advised Mom to avoid romantic entanglements. "Be Careful about those Steady Boy Friends they are Dangerous." My grandfather drew a box around the final word. He asked my mother in another letter, "How is that Old Buck Friend of yours you know you want to watch your step those Boys Get you In Trouble the majority of them Don't have a *heart* So Be Cautious good Luck Your Pop." The boyfriend wasn't my father. "Your Letter sounds good about *Tom* But as you know a Touch of *Love* makes you go Blind use your eyes in the Back of your Head as well as your front ones I Hope He is as you think he is But Be *Careful* I am not saying *Don't* But Just Be Careful."

Mom took her father's advice. She dated Dad after she broke up with Tom but seemed reluctant to commit to another relationship. My mother had a hope chest filled with letters, 4-H journals, livestock ribbons, a pair of faded ballet slippers,

Fig. 2. Mom posing with her trick riding horse Ginger. Author's collection.

Fig. 3. Miss Rocky Ford 1943. Author's collection.

and newspaper clippings. In one letter my father drew a picture of a sad face. "Did you break your date last night? It sure would be nice if I could see you sometime." He later sent her a card that read, "I Love You Terribly ... But I'll Improve With Practice." Dad wrote on the back: "I wish you were here so I could be near you. You have no idea what kind of hell it is when you leave." The message on the next card read, "Women are no damn good!" Dad referred to Mom as "Rosita." He wrote: "I just received your phone call. Woman why do you lead me such a merry chase?" He printed on another card in capital letters: "HOW ARE YOU? YOU GREAT BIG HUNK OF A WOMAN. HAPPY VALENTINE'S DAY." My father confessed: "I don't have much to say. Seems like this weekend was fairly mixed up. Guess I'll sit in my little confused corner and cry." There was an invitation in the hope chest announcing commencement exercises for the class of 1958. A note was enclosed in the envelope. "Dear Rose Mary, Please come to my graduation. I want you to be there to pin on my bars. I hope you will understand this, and try to attend."

My mother seemed to be sending my father mixed signals. She may have been in love, but she was more interested in pursuing her education. Mom became pregnant after the beauty pageant and realized her father was right when he said boyfriends were dangerous. She dropped out of college to marry the man who had already sabotaged her dream to become the next Miss America.

Mom majored in home economics. She planned to move to Paris and become a fashion designer after getting her college degree. Grandma Ethel offered to pay for a backstreet abortion, but Mom decided to have me, even though it meant giving up her fashion career. "That's how much I love you," she said. "I could have had you aborted. But I didn't."

My mother equated love with self-martyrdom. She compared herself to Grandma Ethel, a scrappy fighter who had survived the Depression and who single-handedly ran the car business while raising two children after my grandfather died. Mom admired my grandmother's willingness to pay for an abortion and claimed I didn't appreciate the similar sacrifices she made on my behalf. One day she complained about having to cook my meals and pay for my piano lessons. "Name one thing you've done for me in return." When I hesitated, she said, "Take your time." I heard an imaginary clock tick as the music from *Jeopardy!* played in my head.

I felt responsible for my mother's unhappiness. Every day Dad went to Beman Motors and Son, where he sold cars for Grandma Ethel, while Mom stayed home raising the children she never wanted. Life had dealt my mother a lousy hand. She was stuck with a family and in-laws she couldn't discard. Dad's parents were farmers who lived near Wiley, Colorado. Mom treated them as if they were members of a lower class. They seldom visited our house in Rocky Ford, but when they did, my grandfather would signal he was ready to leave by putting on his hat and waiting by the door. He would whistle a polite tune until my grandmother took the hint.

My mother reserved her greatest scorn for my father's sister, Aunt Sherri. My aunt married a man after high school and moved to a trailer court, where she quickly became pregnant with the first of several children. Mom disliked Sherri because she reminded her of the mistakes she had made in her own life. She wouldn't let Dad pay for chemotherapy when my aunt got breast cancer, so he gave Uncle Kenny money to go to Mexico and purchase Laetrile, a drug that hadn't been approved by the FDA. My uncle confirmed my mother's bleak assessment of her in-laws when he took the funds and ran off with his girlfriend.

Mom opened a ballet academy after Cindi and I started school, then a modeling studio, both of which failed. She served as the state director for a national sewing contest sponsored by the sheep industry entitled "Make It with Wool!" My mother also designed women's clothes and accessories made out of fox fur, raccoon skins, and other semi-exotic animal pelts. The company went bankrupt in less than a year. Her only success occurred when she entered a hat contest organized by the Rocky Ford Ladies' Auxiliary Guild. The other contestants modeled their most elegant apparel. My mother took a different approach. She purchased a battered felt hat at a secondhand store, wired stuffed birds to the top, and squirted glue on the brim to make it look as if the birds had pooped on her head. She attached a sign to the hat that read, "For Some People They Sing!"

Mom won first prize for originality.

My mother had returned to her hometown at the age of nineteen, pregnant and without a college degree. In public she played the cockeyed fatalist who laughed in the face of adversity. She expressed her frustration at home by verbally abusing her husband and children, cursing the town that had served as a stage for her earlier triumphs but that was now a virtual prison.

Mom announced after my grandmother died that she was "all alone in the world." I reminded her she had a brother, and she glared at me as if to imply Uncle Phil didn't count. Her older brother was anointed heir to the car business, which had been rechristened Beman Motors and Son after his birth. My mother had tried to earn her parents' approval by getting

Fig. 4. Grandma Ethel with her children. Author's collection.

good grades and winning a series of beauty pageants, tap dancing contests, and rodeos. But Uncle Phil, the future head of
the family, had been allowed to shirk his responsibilities and
indulge his personal whims.

My uncle looked like the 1950s singing sensation Pat
Boone. He stressed the coincidence by wearing the initials
PB on his monogrammed shirts. His good looks, combined
with his reputation as a bad boy, made him irresistible to
the opposite sex. He impregnated a local girl, who was paid
to leave town. He also dated Peggy Fleming, whom he met
in Colorado Springs at an ice-skating rink. Finally, he wed
my aunt, a former Miss Rodeo America (née Miss Rodeo
Oregon), Rocky Ford's only celebrity.

Uncle Phil had an affair with his secretary after getting
married. When Grandma Ethel died, he withdrew the profits

from the business and absconded to Florida, accompanied by his son, Mike, and his mistress, Louise. Mom was forced to pay the family's debts by selling the business and a small apartment building she had inherited. She used the remaining money to purchase a ranch near Colorado Springs, where we moved in 1971.

My mother continued to resent my father, my sister, and me as well as her parents. Grandma Ethel had favored my uncle, while my grandfather's illness had prevented Mom from attending an Ivy League school. She became increasingly discontented after we moved to the ranch. She contradicted the orders my father gave the foreman and insisted on breaking a stud horse that everyone else considered too dangerous to ride. My mother was determined to prove she was still an expert equestrian. Instead of escaping from Rocky Ford, she was competing with ghosts from her past.

Eventually, I realized my mother was a manic-depressive. Dad dealt with the problem by drinking. Every evening after work he mixed himself a bourbon and coke. He refilled his glass at regular intervals until it was time for bed. My father only lost his temper once. He hit my mother and left the house in a rage. He returned the next day, and the incident was never referred to again.

Mom surprised me one day by confessing she and Dad hadn't had sex since my sister was born. I hated it when she shared the details of her personal life with Cindi and me. She made us stand in the hallway when she went to the bathroom and talked to us through a crack in the door. Once I thought, "This woman has no boundaries." After she and Dad had an argument, Mom said to me, "Remember when you promised to buy me a mink coat and take me dancing?" I pretended not to know what she was talking about.

I didn't like to think of myself as a romantic substitute for my father.

My mother complained about her nonexistent sex life. "Do you know what it's like laying next to a man night after night? Never once—"

"Mom!" I resisted the temptation to cover my ears. "Maybe you should talk to a therapist."

My mother acted as if I had slapped her in the face. "I don't believe in discussing our problems outside the family," she said.

We had gone to a counselor once before. Mom departed the office in tears when my father, my sister, and I accused her of making our lives a living hell. She frequently threatened to get a divorce. But it was Dad who finally left after twenty-five years of abuse. My parents had a troubled relationship. But the longevity of their marriage suggested that for every dominant spouse there was a complementary subordinate spouse. My father was a void, and my mother was nature's way of filling that void.

I realized I had taken Dad for granted. For years he had reacted to Mom's outbursts by withdrawing behind an invisible barrier. If my mother had no boundaries, my father had plenty of them. He was the most self-contained person I knew.

I envied Dad for quitting his marriage. It wasn't as easy for a son to divorce his mother. One year I made mom a Mother's Day card. I printed the words "I love you" on a pink piece of construction paper and wrote a poem to go with it:

Roses are red.
Violets are blue.
Sugar is sweet,
And so are you.

If you love me,
As I love you,
No knife can cut
Our love in two.

Now my father was gone. His love had been cut by something stronger than a knife.

The foreman quit because he claimed he couldn't work for my mother. Mom neglected the chores and allowed the fences to sag, forcing the livestock to fend for themselves. She stopped cleaning the house and sat in her nightgown all day drinking coffee, smoking cigarettes, and playing computer solitaire. My mother bitched about my father during their marriage, but she seemed sad when he was gone. She became depressed when Cindi and I left home for college, yet she wasn't excited when we came back to visit. I spoke to my mother once on the phone about my plans for Christmas vacation. "I guess I'm going to have to pick you up at the airport," she sighed. I suggested I could take a taxi, and she responded by saying she didn't have any food in the house. I asked her if she wanted me to pay the taxi driver to stop at the store. She ignored me and complained about having to wash my sheets and make the bed.

Mom was trying to tell me something I didn't want to hear. I recommended again that she see a therapist.

"I'm too old to change," she said.

Cindi was unsympathetic to our mother's plight. She told me she had been physically abused as a child. My sister described how our mother used to go into her room late at night, make her get out of bed, and pull down her underwear. Then she beat my sister with a leather quirt, whipping her where the marks wouldn't show.

Cindi saw the shocked expression on my face. "Don't you remember the time you talked back to Mom and she washed your mouth out with soap until you threw up in the sink?" I had no recollection of such an incident. But I had other memories, some comical, some not so funny. My mother often wandered around the house when she felt restless, humming the Engelbert Humperdinck song "Please Release Me (Let Me Go)." Once I saw her standing on the reducing machine with the vibrating strap placed around her fanny, reading *The Manchurian Candidate*. On another occasion she pressed the automatic switch in the car and rolled up the window while my arm hung outside. Mom was startled when I screamed. Then she laughed.

My mother used a quirt to herd livestock as a child. Later she hung it on a wall in our house to remind Cindi and me what would happen if we misbehaved. One day, feeling stressed, I stole a cigarette and a lighter from Mom's purse. Then I went to my room and locked the door. I lit the cigarette and placed it between my lips, choking as I inhaled the smoke. When I tossed the cigarette into a wastepaper basket, it burst into flames.

Years later I reminded my sister of this episode from our past. Cindi said: "If you burned down our house, where did we live after that? Were we homeless or what? Tell me. I'd like to know." Although they were logical questions, I was unable to answer them. My memory was like a story. It had a beginning, a middle, and an end. Asking what happened after I burned down our house was like asking what happened to Scarlett after the conclusion of *Gone with the Wind*.

I wondered why I had fabricated such a preposterous story. Maybe I wanted to destroy the prison where my mother held me captive.

Fig. 5. My family at our house on Willow Avenue. Author's collection.

Mom also felt trapped. She blamed Rocky Ford for all her problems. I remembered my hometown as a friendly farming community located in the heartland of rural America. It was a place where children played in the streets, where everyone knew each other and no one locked their doors at night. My mother made Rocky Ford sound like a wasteland filled with desperate inhabitants leading miserable lives.

Small towns were associated with an earlier era of our nation's history. For me they represented America's childhood, a seemingly idyllic, more innocent time. Americans romanticized the rural past in the same nostalgic way adults looked back on their youth. There was less crime in small towns, life was less hectic, and the majority of Americans believed in traditional values. But there was also a tendency to see such places as isolated, backward communities. As more people migrated to metropolitan areas, there came to be a growing perception that rural America had been left in the dust. Small towns were perceived to be economically languishing, populated by inhabitants who were provincial, conservative, suspicious of outsiders, and resistant to change.

I began to question whether my memories of Rocky Ford were accurate. I remembered taking refuge from the summer heat by swimming with friends at the pool. White children didn't go on Sunday, when Hispanic residents used the facility. It was rumored that if you swam with "Mexicans," your body would become covered with grease, causing the water to repel off your skin.

Rocky Ford had a troubled history. During World War II a Japanese American internment camp had been located several miles from town. In addition to racial tensions there were other problems that especially affected members of rural communities. I tried to imagine what it would be like living in Rocky Ford as a gay person, fearful of having one's secret exposed, or feeling stuck in a place where there were few educational or job opportunities. I had a satisfying career in Los Angeles. If I had stayed in Rocky Ford, I might have become depressed like my mother, believing I had wasted my life.

One of my friends in Los Angeles was raised in Rocky Ford and had mixed feelings about our hometown. Greg LaVoi had been two grades ahead of me in school. Our families had both moved to Colorado Springs in the early 1970s. Now he was a costume designer for a hit series on cable TV. As a child, he staged plays in his parents' basement and made costumes for the actors who appeared in his amateur productions. Greg wouldn't have become successful if his family had remained in Rocky Ford. He was a gay version of the fashion designer my mother once hoped to become.

Greg said residents viewed my father as an "outsider." They thought he had seduced the town's favorite daughter to secure a position at Beman Motors and Son. "There was a feeling that your father was riding on your mother's coattails." I knew Dad didn't marry Mom for her money. My grandparents had lost their Studebaker dealership in the 1950s. By the end of the decade they were reduced to selling used cars. But there was no doubt people were proud of Mom. Greg sorted through his mother's belongings after she died and discovered a box of newspapers documenting Mom's career as a teenage beauty queen and trick riding prodigy. I wondered how many other residents had pinned their hopes on my mother and were disappointed when she didn't fulfill her dream.

I became curious to learn more about my hometown after talking to Greg. Was Rocky Ford the pastoral oasis of my youth? Or was it a mirage that had long since evaporated, like thousands of small towns in the American West?

I visited the research library at UCLA in the spring of 2009 and discovered a book in the Special Collections Department entitled *A History of the Arkansas Valley*. Published in 1881, it was typical of the promotional literature meant to entice settlers out West. The author depicted Colorado as "an embodiment of romance" and the valley as a veritable "wonderland."

The region was named after the Arkansas River, which originates in Colorado. It winds its way through the South and empties into the Mississippi River near the dwarf-sized town with the self-aggrandizing name of Napoleon, Arkansas. The area was once considered part of the Great American Desert. Although this designation was misleading, given the river's presence, no one familiar with the place would have described it as a garden of earthly delights. The so-called valley was located on the high plains at an elevation of approximately four thousand feet. The climate was less than ideal for farming. The region received eleven inches of rainfall per year. There were frequent tornadoes, hail and electrical storms, and periodic cycles of drought.

Rocky Ford was founded by a merchant from Illinois named George Washington Swink. In 1871 he built a general store near a shallow crossing on the south side of the river and began growing cantaloupes and watermelons. The fruit required little moisture and adapted well to the arid environment. Swink soon acquired a reputation for producing America's sweetest and most succulent melons. By the end of the nineteenth century he was shipping his harvest to restaurants back east as well as to markets overseas, where Rocky Ford melons sold for four dollars per crate, at the time an astronomical sum.

Historians used Swink's success to illustrate the rise of civilization on the early frontier. Each phase of the town's evolution was treated as a noteworthy milestone, though some seemed modest in retrospect. The Little White School was founded in 1877. Its playground doubled as the town's unofficial cemetery. Rocky Ford also took pride in its two-story outhouse, located in an alley behind the St. James Hotel. The library opened in 1909. It featured a complete edition of Shakespeare's plays and a selection of agricultural manuals. People planted cottonwood trees on Main Street the following year, but horses ate the leaves on the saplings, stripping them bare. Most accounts traced the history of Rocky Ford up to the Great Depression. Afterward the town once known as "The Melon Capital of the World" disappeared from the official record.

Rocky Ford reminded me of my mother. The original settlement was a bustling commercial center. The town later developed into a vital agricultural hub. Its population began to dwindle during the Dust Bowl. When Mom was growing up, it was a shell of its former self.

Wondering what Rocky Ford was like today, I purchased a subscription to the *Daily Gazette*. The paper was published five days each week. The Monday through Thursday editions were four pages long. The Friday edition, which was twice that length, included weekend TV listings and "Church News." The front page was devoted to local news, obituaries, the weather forecast, and measuring charts listing the water levels at the region's irrigation canals. The left-hand column featured national and international news. The right-hand column, entitled "Around Town," offered a mix of gossip, notices about upcoming events, and corrections of earlier articles.

People in Rocky Ford had an insular view of the world. But they also had a strong sense of community pride. One day the paper published an article about a grade-schooler who had won a trophy for good citizenship. When a resident experienced any sort of misfortune, neighbors rallied to support the person in need. The townspeople were linked together by intimacy and mutual interest, ties that were strengthened during times of adversity.

There were also disadvantages living in a small town such as Rocky Ford. No one had any privacy. The *Daily Gazette* identified residents who were fined for failing to water their yards. Car crashes accounted for a surprising percentage of the region's fatalities because motorists often drove recklessly on rural roads. Occasionally, someone died as a result of a freak occurrence, like the son of a farmer who was killed in "an agriculturally related accident" when he suffocated after falling into a grainery bin.

Several stores on Main Street had closed due to the recession. The owner of Don's Men's Store installed a security gate after his establishment was burglarized twice in a two-year period. The Tank 'n' Tummy was robbed by a teenage Hispanic male armed with a gun. Another man broke into the store overnight and was captured on videotape hauling off twenty-three cartons of Marlboro cigarettes in a plastic bag.

Residential neighborhoods were also affected by the economic downturn. Many were littered with "derelict buildings, broken windows, and trash," according to one concerned citizen who complained to the *Daily Gazette*. The writer had moved from Denver to escape from urban blight. He didn't regret his decision but claimed Rocky Ford "needed to work on improving itself."

I thought about writing a book that traced the history of my hometown from its promising origin to the present, hoping it might help me understand my mother's depression. I was about to begin my summer sabbatical and realized I could return to Rocky Ford in time for the fair. I logged onto the Internet and discovered this year's theme was "We Are a SLICE of the Valley." The manager was a woman named Sally Cope. She mentioned in her online bio that she had once modeled for Rose Mary Allmendinger, "a former resident of Rocky Ford."

I emailed Sally and told her I was coming back to research a book. She replied that she had fond memories of my mother and recommended I contact Nancy Aschermann, the superintendent of schools. I told Nancy that Mrs. Arline Fox, my fourth-grade teacher, had inspired me to become a professor. I referred to Mrs. Fox in the past tense, and she emailed me several hours later to let me know she was still very much alive. The octogenarian described herself as a lifelong liberal. She complained that Rocky Ford was "full of Republicans" and described how her neighbors had been shocked when she purchased a Prius. "No one in this damn town believes in global warming."

Nevertheless, Mrs. Fox sounded happy living in Rocky Ford. She suggested I contact another former student, Matt Mendenhall, who owned a vacation house in town. Matt told me his family had moved to Williams, Arizona, in 1972. He said Williams seemed like a "pit" compared to "pretty, well-groomed" Rocky Ford. Eventually, his hometown became "a 'mythical place' in my mind." Matt returned there on holidays and hung out in his basement, composing music and playing video games.

Matt reminded me of Greg, who had spent his childhood putting on plays. For these two gay men the basement was a closet, a place where they were free to pursue their private passions. They admired the historic buildings on Main Street but had little contact with the town's other residents. Matt admitted the "real" Rocky Ford was a turbulent place in the 1960s. His father, the high school principal, had mediated a series of conflicts between Chicanos and whites. His older brother, a "hippie," was arrested by the police for reasons he didn't specify.

Matt asked if I was haunted by a "sense of 'otherness' not uncommon for rural gay kids." As a child, he had felt different from other people and yearned to be part of a larger community. He kept returning to Rocky Ford as an adult, searching for something that wasn't there. Matt wrote: "When you and I were boys this town supported four car dealerships, three bakeries, and a number of clothing stores. Now Main Street is all but abandoned. What I like about this town as a retreat (I wouldn't want to work here and learn to hate the pettiness that contaminates everyday life) are the trees, the houses, and the obvious care with which the town was built. I've sat on my backyard deck and felt lucky being here while at the same time being keenly aware that on another given deck someone else was feeling isolated and miserable."

I told Matt I hadn't been aware of my sexuality at the time. Later Cindi challenged that statement. "Even I knew you were gay." She recalled how I played with my troll doll and "ran like a girl." Our father got angry one day when we raced in the yard and she beat me.

I wondered if returning to Rocky Ford was a good idea. I had reconnected with people who remembered my family and had been offered a place to stay while in town. I hoped by the end of the summer I wouldn't be one of those people Matt imagined sitting on the porch by himself.

Cindi said she wouldn't come see me because she didn't want to revisit the past. I became uneasy when a colleague told me she looked forward to hearing about my trip to "Rocky Road." I corrected her, and she apologized for her slip of the tongue.

I landed at Denver International Airport on August 9, 2009, took a shuttle to the rental agency, picked up my car, and headed south on I-25. Midway through Pueblo I exited east on Highway 50. I detected a change in the scenery as I journeyed toward my destination. The fast-food restaurants and self-service gas stations slowly disappeared as I entered the countryside. I noticed a John Deere dealership and a cement factory sitting next to a mountain of gravel. A farmhouse yard was littered with spools of barbed wire, piles of discarded tires, and rusting farm machinery. The property gave way to rows of corn and fields of alfalfa.

I became bored by the landscape and turned on the radio. A preacher's voice exhorted listeners to repent their sins. A country music station featured a singer wailing a depressing refrain. On another station a conservative talk show host criticized the government's stance on immigration reform.

I passed a caution sign that showed a picture of a farmer driving a tractor. The sign read, "Share the Road with Others." I stared at the yellow dashes on the asphalt. A pool of water materialized on the highway in front of me. As I approached, it evaporated and reappeared several miles ahead.

I wondered if I had made a mistake. Instead of coming home, I felt like I was entering a shadowy realm filled with ghosts from my past.

I arrived at dusk on the outskirts of town. A traffic light flashed red on Main Street. Vacant, weed-strewn lots appeared on the street like gaps in a smile. I crossed the railroad tracks and recognized the chamber of commerce, a feedstore that had gone out of business, and the Grand movie theater. Some of the older homes were in pristine condition, while others languished in neglect. The downspouts were detached from their gutters, and the screen doors were frayed at the edges. The houses faded in the deepening gloom.

I turned left on Tennyson Drive and crept down a one-block street to a one-story house with a light in the living room window. A woman in her eighties greeted me with a smile when I knocked on the door. I stepped across the threshold and hugged Mrs. Fox, feeling like a child again. She returned

Fig. 6. Rocky Ford's only movie theater, 2009. Courtesy Lex
Nichols Photography.

my embrace and led me into the kitchen, where she fixed me
a drink.

I was surprised she would offer one of her former students
alcohol. Then I remembered I was no longer a ten-year-old
boy. I asked Mrs. Fox if she kept in touch with my classmates.
She told me Chris Claycomb was blind and lived with his
mother. "He always had bad eyesight, even as a child." Lynn
Dickie had gotten married and moved to Texas. "Her father
and I play Scrabble sometimes." Mrs. Fox winked at me.
"He's a Democrat too." Then she said: "Carl Zimmerman
got divorced. Someone saw him driving a red sports car the
other day."

Forty years ago Mrs. Fox had taught me the multiplication
tables. Now I was drinking bourbon on her living room couch.
Recalling how Mrs. Fox had entertained her students by playing Disney tunes on an upright piano, I started singing "Never

Smile at a Crocodile" from *Peter Pan*. Mrs. Fox looked at my empty glass. "Let's go see Matt's house, shall we?"

She went outside and got in her Prius, and I followed in my car as she turned onto Main Street. After driving a block and a half, she parked in front of a three-story bungalow that had been renovated to showcase its original charm. She fumbled in the dark, attempting to fit a key in the lock, then opened the door and flipped on a switch. Mrs. Fox gave me a tour of the house. After she left I walked into the kitchen, where a sliding glass door led to a deck in the backyard. My senses adjusted to the darkness. I smelled manure coming from a feedlot east of town. In the distance I heard a train whistle. It grew louder, reaching a crescendo. Slowly, almost imperceptibly, it faded away.

The cicadas in the locust trees began singing in unison. I remembered playing in our yard on Willow Avenue. One day I discovered an object clinging to the bark of a tree. I ran inside to show my mother, and she told me it was the exoskeleton of a baby cicada. After a female cicada mated, she deposited her egg on a twig. Later it hatched, and the newborn insect dropped to the ground, burrowing itself into the earth. It completed its metamorphosis by shedding its skin when it reemerged from the soil.

Looking at the shriveled husk in my hand, I imagined the cicada breaking out of its shell and testing its wings in the sun before flying away.

CHAPTER TWO

TJ Is a Wonderful Boy

The next morning brought me back to reality. Realizing my return to farm country had triggered my allergies, I stumbled into the bathroom and took a Claritin-D. Then I went to the grocery store to buy food for breakfast.

Next door to the store was the post office. It had been built during the Depression and paid tribute to the town's illustrious past. The neoclassical edifice featured a portico supported by stately white columns and an impressive staircase leading up to the door. In the lobby was a mural entitled *The First Crossing at Rocky Ford*. Swink appeared riding across the Arkansas River on horseback, leading his wife, who sat in a covered wagon accompanied by their pet dog. (She actually arrived several years later by train.) The muddy water had been transformed into a sparkling stream. In the background stood an inviting grove of cottonwood trees. The sky was upholstered with fluffy white clouds.

Swink began his career selling provisions to settlers. The food market was a less successful version of his general store.

THE FIRST CROSSING AT ROCKY FORD.

Fig. 7. Mural in the Rocky Ford Post Office, painted by Victor Higgins in 1936. Photo courtesy Lex Nichols Photography.

It was made out of cinder blocks and had a cheap metal roof. The checkout lady told me that nowadays most people shopped at the Wal-Mart in nearby La Junta.

After eating breakfast, I decided to visit the chamber of commerce, which was housed in the former depot of the Santa Fe Railroad. The original depot had been replaced in 1907 by a building with carved gables and a Venetian tile roof, signifying Rocky Ford's importance at the turn of the century. The chamber of commerce took over the depot when the railroad discontinued its service to Rocky Ford in 1979. It supported local businesses by selling "melon money," which could be exchanged for goods at participating stores. The receptionist said the organization had abandoned the program due to the recent recession.

Main Street resembled a ghost town. A sign on the door of a barbershop said "Open/Abierto." There was a thrift store that sold used clothes and secondhand furniture. Next to the store was a real estate agency. I peered through the glass into its empty interior.

The former headquarters for Beman Motors and Son stood at the corner of Main Street and Elm. The Colorado State

Fig. 8. Rocky Ford during its heyday, date unknown. Author's collection.

Employment Agency had moved into the building after the car dealership went out of business. It was currently occupied by the First National Bank. I entered the premises, and the teller looked crestfallen when she realized I wasn't a customer. I told her who my grandfather was. She didn't recognize his name, even though it appeared in raised brick letters on the building's exterior.

There was a mural painted on a wall next to a vacant lot at the other end of the block. *A Short History of Rocky Ford* chronicled the evolution of the American West. In the first panel a herd of buffalo grazed on a prairie. Subsequent scenes depicted an Indian, a cowboy twirling a rope, a farmer sprinkling seeds on the ground, a bank and a church, an airplane, and a laptop computer. The mural preserved the official myth of Rocky Ford. My hometown was no longer a center of farming and industry. Its population had decreased by 20 percent

Fig. 9. My grandfather's former car dealership. Courtesy Lex
Nichols Photography.

in the last fifty years. Twice as many residents lived below the
poverty level compared to people in other parts of the state.

A number of establishments had gone out of business,
including Loyd's Lovely Lady, the Hair Affair, and a store with
no name. Its windows were covered with classified ads from
the *Rocky Mountain News* dated October 13, 2005.

Mom had appeared on the front page of the same paper
forty-nine years earlier, while attending the National Stock
Show in Denver. The caption read, "Girl from Golden West."
Next to my mother was an article reporting the details of
Shelley Winters's latest divorce. A headline was emblazoned
across the top of the page. "SLUM CLEARANCE PLAN SENT
TO MAYOR."

Mom wasn't a movie star with a sensational personal life.
She was a young girl from a small town in Colorado, a rep-
resentative of an earlier era, a reminder that there had once

Fig. 10. A glimpse into Rocky Ford's past. Courtesy Lex Nichols Photography.

been a West without cities and slums. I gazed at the papers plastered on the window next door to Loyd's Lovely Lady and imagined her face staring back at me.

The building next to another vacant lot had formerly been used as a billboard. It had been repainted each time someone put a new ad on the wall. The surface paint had peeled away like a palimpsest, revealing successive layers underneath. I noticed the phrase "Open Kettle Pure Lard," the letters N-U-C-K-O-L-L-S, and the fragment "Bakery and Grocery St— ." *A Short History of Rocky Ford* presented a progressive version of history. But the billboard enabled viewers to travel backward in time. Each excavated level of sediment exposed another piece of the past.

An antique shop catered to customers who collected memorabilia. A gramophone was playing the ragtime melody "Solace" when I walked in the door. There were watermelons embroidered on dish towels, tea cozies, egg warmers, linen, pillows, and quilts.

An Underwood typewriter sat on a rolltop desk. Someone had placed a piece of paper between the roller and the crossbar and typed a sentence in capital letters: NOW IS THE TIME FOR ALL GOOD MEN TO COME TO THE AID OF THE PARTY. Underneath the sentence someone (else?) had typed: TJ IS A WONDERFUL BOY.

My mother had a hope chest filled with trophies and ribbons. She had been Rocky Ford's golden girl, but I wondered if she had ever been loved. Her parents were dead, her husband had left her, and she had alienated her children by treating them unkindly. I wished Mom had written those words about me.

I left the store in a pensive mood and went next door to the pharmacy. The previous owner's daughter Kellie had been a classmate of mine. I remembered when we played at her house we had to be quiet because her mother was "resting" upstairs. Mrs. Fox told me Mrs. Harris suffered from depression. Her son had had some sort of mysterious ailment and had died after our family left Rocky Ford.

One day Kellie made a ring out of thread and asked me to stick my finger inside the loop next to hers. Then we broke the thread by pulling our fingers apart, which was what Kellie said adults did on their wedding night. Kellie sent me a nude photograph after my family moved to the ranch. I destroyed it and never wrote back. Now I realized Kellie had been lonely. She had lost her brother, and her mother was a recluse. I couldn't give Kellie what she needed. I had never been loved and didn't know how to love in return.

I entered Don's Men's Store when I noticed the security gate was unlocked. The owner nodded when I told him my name. "I thought you looked like a Beman." Don described my grandfather as a generous man. He had extended credit to customers during the Depression and traded cars to Indians in exchange for animal pelts. Once he raffled a Studebaker, selling tickets for a dollar apiece, and threw a party on the night of the drawing.

I asked Don if he remembered my grandmother. He paused for a moment. Then he said, "Ethel was a pretty shrewd businesswoman." Don changed the subject, telling me that a family had purchased my grandparents' house and moved it to the north side of town. I was unable to locate the house, so I drove to my family's former home on Willow Avenue. The residence stood on an acre of land. In the backyard was an orchard with crabapple trees.

As I sat in the car, I remembered that I had once written my mother a note telling her I was running away from home. I ran into the orchard, crawled under a fence, and hid in my neighbors' backyard. She eventually came outside, and my heart beat rapidly as she called my name. I knew she would find me, but I wondered how long it would take.

The next morning I interviewed Sally Cope at the fairgrounds. I noticed workers unloading sound equipment, mechanics assembling carnival rides, volunteers erecting a refreshment tent sponsored by Coors, and high school students armed with spears and plastic bags picking up trash. A woman made a note on her clipboard each time a vehicle passed through the gate.

I recognized Sally even though forty years had passed since she modeled Mom's fur accessories for *Seventeen* magazine. My mother posed for *Vogue* the same year in Central City, a mining town once known as "The Richest Square Mile

Fig. 11. Rocky Ford's original grandstand, 1919. Author's collection.

on Earth." Mom was photographed next to an abandoned mine shaft in a hot-pink pantsuit and sleeveless fur vest. The caption read: "Wild fur — langorous [*sic*] long hairs — wolf and raccoon. Wear them and give life to a ghost town or light up the night like a meteor." The words were prophetic. My mother's career as a fashion designer ended with her appearance in *Vogue*. Her business went bankrupt, and she returned to Rocky Ford, a victim of the West's boom-bust economy.

The annual fair started in 1878. Otero County no longer subsidized the event due to a shortage of government funds. The city relied on donations from residents and corporations such as Coors and CenturyTel. Sally received a small salary for organizing the fair, booking live entertainment, and coordinating the parade and the rodeo. Initially, Swink used the fair to disprove the notion that the valley was fit "only for steers and coyotes." Farmers exhibited their crops in the Alfalfa Palace. Each year they built walls with hay bales and made a roof out of straw. It was eventually replaced by a permanent structure, though there were now fewer crops on display.

The Roundhouse showcased the arts and crafts exhibit.

A reporter for the *Rocky Ford Enterprise*, the town's first newspaper, cataloged the entries submitted in 1901. The list included "crazy quilts, paintings on velvet, fancy knit stockings, wrought undergarments, gentlemen's shirts, slipper cases, hair work, and sideboarded scarves." This year there were only a handful of entries.

Volunteers had spent the last year raising money to renovate the Roundhouse. One of them told me children threw rocks at the windows when they cut through the fairgrounds on their way home from school. Although the building was an architectural gem, it sat empty most of the year. It was a tempting target for young people who had no sense of history and community pride.

Residents were also restoring the horse stalls. I told a man how inspiring it was to see volunteers donating their time to rebuild the adobe ruins.

"They're mostly tree huggers from Boulder," he said.

They were people like me looking for a way to reconnect with the past.

The original grandstand seated four thousand people. It was the largest freestanding structure in the valley when it was erected in 1903. In 1968 it caught fire and burned to the ground. One resident at the time wrote a letter to the *Daily Gazette* suggesting the accident was a "blessing in disguise." Rocky Ford should stop celebrating the past because it was no longer the "old wild west." But the town chose to continue the fair and replaced the grandstand with a smaller, fireproof facility the following year.

I remembered playing with Cindi in the grandstand one summer after the fair. We ran up and down the bleachers, frightened by the sound of our echoing footsteps. The horse stalls were empty, and the toilets were buzzing with flies. There were weeds growing in the bull pens and calf-roping chutes.

I admired Sally for trying to preserve Rocky Ford's traditions. She had married a farmer after modeling for Mom, supplemented her income by selling Mary Kay cosmetics, and taught a 4-H seminar called "Sewing and Decorating Your Duds." My mother, who had greater ambitions, wrote an essay on leadership in high school. "During my four years in home economics I have broadened myself in a great many ways." Mom believed the education she received in Rocky Ford would prepare her for success in the outside world. It saddened me to know what the future held in store. When she looked back on her achievements, she concluded, "Utter contentment and sheer satisfaction have been my rewards."

I interviewed Carroll and Millie Donelson in the afternoon. They were the former owners of Ustick Funeral Home. Carl Ustick, Millie's grandfather, started the business in 1913. Carl Jr. inherited the mortuary, then handed it over to his daughter and her husband, who passed it on to their son.

It was ironic that the town's most successful business was

a funeral home. Millie admitted a lot of young folks had fled Rocky Ford. But an influx of retirees had taken their place, attracted by the peaceful lifestyle and low cost of living. They were also living longer due to advances in medicine. "We don't have as many funerals as you might imagine," said Millie.

Carroll claimed, "Rocky Ford will never die."

Although he was optimistic, the lower death rate meant less business for the funeral home. Carroll's son had sold the mortuary in 2008. The new owner modernized the operation to attract more customers. People could purchase tributes to their loved ones on DVD, plan their own funerals, and purchase caskets online. Obituaries were published on the mortuary's website. (A recommended link there led me to the Center for Loss and Life Transition, which specialized in guiding mourners through "their unique life journeys.") The industry dealt with death more efficiently in the twenty-first century. The Donelsons had befriended the clients who paid for their services and took pride in helping them make it through a difficult time in their lives. Nowadays people enrolled in virtual seminars to cope with their grief.

I remembered an obituary from 1899 I had read in the *Enterprise*. When a sixteen-year-old girl named Lottie Williams died, her classmates decorated her desk with flowers and bows. The reporter wrote, "A gloom like a pall rests on the school, and the children greet each other with hushed voices, knowing that in her death they have lost a true friend and loving companion." Life was precious on the early frontier. Rocky Ford was a small community in which each death represented a significant loss. I wondered if residents took death for granted now — if they had given up on their town.

On Wednesday I went to a senior citizens pageant at the community center. The contestants were parked in wheelchairs at one end of the room. The reigning Silver King and Queen, wearing mantels made of Christmas tinsel, were placed in the middle. An elderly pianist and a harmonica player warmed up the audience. Sally's mother, B. J. Thomas, and her friend Amy Konishi frequently performed at similar events as well as at funerals. Sally claimed her mother's hobby kept her active, reminding me, "Funerals are for the living."

The emcee introduced the male contestants after the two women had finished performing. Each man gave his name, age, and former occupation. They described a memorable moment in their lives and specified a prize they would like to receive if they were crowned the next Silver King. Howard Amerine had been the valley's "Wonder Bread Man" for seventeen years. When asked to recall the most memorable moment in his life, he answered, "Watching the atom bombs being dropped on Japan." Rito Sarmiento once shook hands with Nixon. Erva Thaxton recalled going to school with the actor who played Festus on *Gunsmoke*. One contestant asked for a coupon to eat at the Red Lobster in Pueblo if he won.

The women put on a talent show. Maxine Freemyer brought some popcorn she had made at her retirement home. Ruth Sanders displayed a sample of her embroidery work. Roberta Tolby shared a poem she had written entitled "Believe in Yourself." Clara Chamberlin performed a routine she had learned in her exercise class. Her physical therapist put a cassette in a boom box, and the contestant rotated her shoulders in sync with the music. Leta Manchego sang "God Bless America" in Spanish while her great-great-grandchildren waved miniature American flags. During her performance a train rumbled past the chamber of commerce. It drowned out her voice as it tooted its whistle and continued through town.

I clapped as Mrs. Chamberlin danced in her wheelchair

and cheered when Mrs. Manchego finished her song. These were decent people with unremarkable talents and modest dreams. But the community was there to support them. The pageant was a celebration of life.

After the contest I went to the El Capitan to speak to the Rotary Club. It had once been the fanciest restaurant in town. Now it looked like it needed a facelift. Peeling paint covered the building like wrinkled skin. In the lobby I recognized the same crimson wallpaper from my childhood, the same fake Victorian furniture, the same reproduction oil paintings, and the same potted plants, their plastic leaves coated with dust.

Nancy Aschermann introduced me to Russell Van Dyk. He told me his father was my next-door neighbor. Nancy identified other members of the Rotary Club at our table, including a florist, the owner of the *Daily Gazette*, a Swedish exchange student, and the director of the retirement home.

Russell called the meeting to order. A minister thanked God for the food we were about to eat. Then we recited the Pledge of Allegiance and sang "My Country 'Tis of Thee" while facing a flag that hung on the wall. During lunch I spoke about my research project and experienced the same connection with the audience I had felt at the community center. Suspecting some members of the Rotary Club had known my parents and grandparents, I asked if I could interview them while I was visiting town. The owner of a local repair shop told me his wife had been friends with my mother in school and invited me to stop by his house after work. J. R. Thompson, the owner of the *Daily Gazette*, offered to help me with my research by allowing me to inspect the newspaper's files.

Before the meeting adjourned, we sang a selection from the Rotarian songbook entitled "Sing, Ev'ryone, Sing."

Let's get together in all kinds of
Weather and sing, ev'ryone, sing.
Smile, ev'ryone, smile. Smile, ev'ryone, smile.
All of your troubles will vanish like bubbles,
So smile, ev'ryone, smile.

J. R. Thompson offered me a packet of seeds as I left the restaurant. The cover read:

Thank You
from your friends at the
Rocky Ford Rotary Club
Rocky Ford, Colorado, USA
The melon capital of the world!

The seeds were a gift from the organization's goodwill ambassador, a token of fellowship, a symbol of hope. They represented a dream that continued to thrive.

The next day I attended a baby contest at the fairgrounds. The contest originated in 1913 and was intended to demonstrate that farmers could produce healthy human offspring, not just "livestock, fruits and vegetables, poultry, and hogs." A newspaper editorial suggested parents should nurture their infants like crops. Outlining the principles of a new science known as "eugenics," the writer emphasized wholesome living and good nutrition as key ingredients in a child's development.

There was a high infant mortality rate on the western frontier. Children often succumbed to the region's harsh climate and dangerous living conditions. Those who survived were expected to take care of their younger siblings and work on the farm. I was a sickly and temperamental infant who wouldn't have lasted long on the plains. One of my baby pictures showed me sleeping in my crib. My rib cage poked through my skin, and the diaper was too big for my waist. In another photograph I cried as I sucked on my fist. Mom was unable to breastfeed me. I wondered if I was scared of her. She told Cindi and me she wished we had never been born. Once I sat on her lap while she read to me. She became upset when I leaned against her pillowy breasts. "Don't touch those," she said.

When I was older, I worried Mom wouldn't feed me. She hated cooking. Food appeared on the table at irregular intervals like sullen acknowledgments of a duty she was contractually forced to perform.

I never went hungry as a child. But I had an emptiness my mother was unable to fill.

That night I had dinner with Mrs. Fox, her daughter, Ann, and her son-in-law, Kent, who were in town for the fair. They were concerned about Rocky Ford's decline. J. R. Thompson had claimed in an editorial it didn't do any good to dwell on the negative. Kent said, "I can't go along with that." Mrs. Fox had canceled her subscription to the *Daily Gazette* when the owner endorsed John McCain for president. She and her liberal friends often asked each other, "Have you read the newspaper yet?" They made fun of the fact it was only four pages long.

I went to a bar after dinner with Ann and Kent. It was a watering hole for misfits and loners. Several people were smoking outside, their faces illuminated by a neon Coors sign hanging over the door. A patron glanced up from his glass, then lowered his head as we entered the room.

A Hispanic man in a booth was talking to himself. Ann said he had fallen in love in the 1960s with a white girl whose father was a prominent businessman. The father forced his daughter to end the relationship. Then the young man was drafted to fight in the Vietnam War. When he returned to Rocky Ford, he was diagnosed with post-traumatic stress disorder. He lived on welfare and spent most evenings at the bar.

Ann finished her story as a band came onstage. The singer performed "A Thousand Miles from Nowhere," accompanied by a drummer and a man playing a steel guitar.

A woman at another table noticed me staring at the gash on her cheek. She explained that she and her daughter had been returning from Ordway on Highway 71 when the car in front of them slammed on its brakes. Her daughter rear-ended the driver, causing them to flip upside down as they flew over his car, landing on the roof of their vehicle. A highway patrol officer scraped the woman's face on the asphalt when he dragged her from the car. "That's how I got this road rash." She picked a bit of gravel out of the wound.

Every evening the tornado siren sounded at seven o'clock. Residents retreated inside, closing their windows and bolting their doors as they prepared for a possible storm. After dark the town assumed a slightly sinister character. Only people who were bored or lonely ventured outside. Once a motorist screamed "Faggot!" when he saw Matt on the street.

The customers in the bar were seeking refuge in each other's company. We had bruises on our memories, like the country singer said. Heartaches in our pockets and echoes in our heads.

On Friday morning residents converged on Main Street to watch the parade. Homeowners moved their cars an hour beforehand so spectators could place their folding chairs next to the curb. Others opened their garages and served donuts and coffee or chatted with their neighbors as they sat on their lawns.

I felt detached as people gathered around me. I remembered when my family had entered the parade to represent Beman Motors and Son. Although the parade was intended to rally the community, it reminded me how I didn't fit in. Uncle Phil and Aunt Vicki were supposed to ride in a covered wagon while my cousin, my sister, and I followed on horseback. Everyone knew how to ride except me. Mom tried to remedy the situation before the parade by purchasing a Shetland pony named Nicker and giving me lessons at my uncle's farm. Unfortunately, Nicker disliked me from the instant we met. He opened his mouth when I offered him a sugar cube, and I reacted like Little Red Riding Hood marveling at what big teeth her grandmother had. When I mounted my pony, he dilated his nostrils and laid back his ears. Sometimes he bucked, forcing me to cling to the saddle horn. Once he tore into a gallop, running alongside a barbed wire fence and ripping my pants to shreds as I tried to extricate my feet from the stirrups.

I couldn't decide whom I hated more, Nicker or my mother. Every time I fell, she insisted I climb back in the saddle to show the horse who was boss. I didn't sleep the night before the parade because I worried Nicker would kill me on the way into town. I imagined him darting in front of an oncoming car. Perhaps he would lie on the ground like he was taking a bath and crush me as he rolled in the dirt.

We left Uncle Phil's house the next morning. Nicker took a few steps, then stopped. I kicked him in the ribs when he refused to budge. He noticed some weeds in a ditch and moseyed over to nibble them, ignoring me when I tugged on the reins. He started moving, then halted again, feigning horror when he spotted a stick in the road that looked like a snake.

I was afraid my family would leave me behind. They must have come to my rescue, but I didn't remember that part of the story. I associated the parade with my childhood fear of abandonment.

Many people had deserted Rocky Ford. There was less solidarity among the remaining citizens. Mrs. Fox mocked the parade as it came down Main Street. Four police cars and an ambulance led the procession. A fire engine filled with children waved to the crowd.

"Can you believe it?" said Mrs. Fox. "Four cop cars, and they can't catch anyone."

A man drove a John Deere fertilizer-insecticide sprayer. A small group of people sat in the back of a flatbed truck. A passenger held a sign that read: "Welcome Class of '79."

Jerre Swink, the town founder's oldest descendant, passed by in a car. Mrs. Fox chuckled, "There goes the last of the Swinks."

The parade included a tribute to the Hispanic community. A deejay sitting in a U-Haul played rap records on a portable console. A motorist followed with the words "Our Lady of Guadalupe" spray-painted on the hood of his car. A mother and father pulled their daughter in a wagon with bows on its wheels. The predominantly white audience that lived on the south side of town responded with scattered applause. Rocky Ford had changed since the 1960s. There was no more Beman Motors and Son, and whites were now a minority.

A couple approached me as the crowd dispersed. The woman identified herself as Mrs. Claycomb. Her eyes gleamed with a malicious intelligence, and a voice warned me to be on my guard.

"You remember Chris," she said. I acknowledged my former fourth-grade classmate. He stared at me through his glasses, wilting me with his impersonal gaze.

Mrs. Claycomb asked how my mother was. Before I could reply, she said, "Rose Mary sure was a living doll." Her voice softened in recollection. Then it hardened again. "Unlike her brother."

Mrs. Claycomb recalled how my grandparents used to receive a shipment of cars every December. Grandma Ethel soaped the showroom windows to prevent residents from viewing them until after the holidays. She let Uncle Phil drive one of the cars and flaunt it in front of people who couldn't afford to buy a new vehicle. "Everyone hated Sonny," Mrs. Claycomb said. Residents used the sarcastic nickname to refer to the heir of Beman Motors and Son.

Ann interrupted us and apologized to Mrs. Claycomb for dragging me away. "You looked like you needed to be rescued," she said as we walked away.

Mrs. Claycomb had described my mother as a "living doll." I remembered a picture of Mom dressed like a cowgirl, posing as Miss Rocky Ford. In another photograph she appeared as Miss Arkansas Valley, wearing a rhinestone tiara on the brim of her hat. Mom looked comfortable in front of the camera, but I suspected each image was calculated to produce an effect. One picture revealed my mother sitting in the saddle with her pet cocker spaniel. Their faces were turned toward the lens. Other photographs showed her performing as a ballerina, strutting as a chorus girl in a high school play, tap dancing with a jazz combo, and competing with other beauty contestants at her college sorority.

Mom told a reporter for the *Rocky Mountain News* in 1967 that contestants in the "Make It with Wool!" pageant should be "a perfect size 10." My mother had an hourglass figure like the Hollywood sex symbols from the 1950s and '60s. Her career as a model ended when magazines started hiring thinner women like Twiggy.

Mom turned to food for consolation and put on weight as the problems in her marriage grew worse. She gnawed on her steak bones, talked with her mouth full of potatoes, and licked her fingers instead of using a napkin. She unbuttoned her pants when she plopped down in the La-Z-Boy and reached under her blouse to release the hooks on her bra. The straps bit into her back as her breasts became heavier, leaving indentation marks on her skin.

Cindi was a picky eater. Maybe it was her way of rebelling against our mother. Mom made her sit at the table every mealtime until she finished her food.

Once Uncle Phil got drunk and tried to kiss my sister. Mom blamed Cindi and cut off her hair. It was the day before we had our photographs taken at school. I wondered if my mother was competing with Cindi. People in Rocky Ford adored my mother and detested Uncle Phil. The residents of this struggling community identified with Mom as an underdog. She was the town's former beauty queen, the less favored child of her parents.

I couldn't ride a horse as well as my mother. Yet Cindi believed Mom loved me more than her. There were lots of photographs of me in her hope chest but none of my sister. Perhaps my mother didn't see me as a threat. Or maybe she embraced my failure and reserved a special place in her heart for me.

On Saturday morning I interviewed Jerre Swink, the last link to the region's glorious past.

My host assumed I wanted to learn more about his great-grandfather, but I was more interested in talking to Jerre. He had survived the Dust Bowl and World War II. I assumed he had plenty of stories tell.

My request took Jerre by surprise. He paused for a moment, then recalled how his parents had tried to get him to marry their neighbor when he came back from the war. The woman was a history teacher. Jerre said, "I didn't care much for history."

That was the end of the story. I had come here to interview one of the town's oldest residents only to discover he "didn't care much for history."

His wife, Midge, removed a teapot from the china cabinet. She told me it was a wedding present from Jerre's grandfather. For years the teapot gave her nightmares. "I was so afraid I would break it," she said.

I was concerned about living up to Mom's reputation, but my hosts had a more difficult task. They were responsible for preserving the Swink family's legacy.

Swink's reputation as a farmer and entrepreneur had grown throughout the early twentieth century. Rocky Ford began to dwindle after his death, and by 2009 there was little left to preserve. The town's founder had held a watermelon feast the first year he produced a bountiful crop. Twenty-five people had accepted Swink's invitation. The farmer sliced melons on the floor of a boxcar and distributed the fruit to his guests. Within three years the crowd had quadrupled in size. Swink built a banquet table and sent visitors home on the train with two coach loads of melons.

In 1894 twelve thousand people attended the fair. Special excursion trains arrived at the depot on Watermelon Day filled to capacity. Disembarking passengers were greeted

Fig. 12. After the feast. Author's collection.

by a marching brass band and escorted to the fairgrounds, where they dined on a pile of melons two hundred feet long and thirty feet wide. In 1897 a reporter described the feast as a gluttonous free-for-all. Swink hired men with butcher knives to carve "the crimson-cored beauties in half. If a melon was found not to be up to his standards, it was thrown under the table and another twenty-five pounder was slashed into hemispheres. After the feast the grove was strewn with the gory remains of half-eaten melons, the result of many sharp appetites."

The Rotary Club expected to distribute two thousand melons this year, fewer than in the past. The governor traditionally opened the pile, cutting the ribbon and handing melons to fairgoers. Jerre Swink was now the master of ceremonies. He was a minor celebrity compared to the governor.

Some of my favorite events had been canceled, including the Watermelon Derby, a marathon that originated in the 1950s. Jockeys crossed the Arkansas River on horseback, raced into town, and entered the fairgrounds, trying not to drop the

Fig. 13. Melon Derby, circa 1950s. Author's collection.

melons they carried under their arms. Rocky Ford shortened the race in 1960. The new rules required contestants to ride four times around the fairgrounds racetrack, changing mounts at the end of each lap.

Uncle Phil and a friend sponsored an entry in 1967. They supplied the horses and hired a jockey, who finished almost two seconds ahead of his nearest competitor. Everyone in my family remembered the episode differently. My cousin claimed Aunt Vicki had trained the horses in a field near their house. The plowed soil made it harder for the horses to gain traction and strengthened their legs. Cindi claimed Mom rode the horses and made them pull wagons to build their endurance. Mike told me the jockey was a man named Butch Morgan. My sister said Uncle Phil used a child. He transferred the rider from one mount to the next so the jockey didn't lose his grip on the melon.

The Watermelon Derby ended several decades ago. It was

a distant memory, like the town that had once been the pride of the valley. All that remained was an uncertain legacy — some apocryphal stories and a fragmented family that couldn't agree who deserved credit for winning the race.

In the afternoon I went to the rodeo. Like the derby, it was part of the history of the American West, a sport that originated among cowboys on the early frontier. The grandstand was practically empty. Sally said the rodeo wasn't as popular as the demolition derby, the feature attraction scheduled for later that night.

I returned in the evening and parked my car at the El Capitan. A teenager passed me in the dark as I walked to the fairgrounds, greeting me with a taunt in his voice. "What's up, bro?"

The fairgrounds bore little resemblance to the scene of my youth. I remembered the year Governor Love had flown down from Denver to open the watermelon pile. I watched his helicopter descend from the sky and felt like a munchkin welcoming Glinda the Good Witch as she landed in Oz.

The children's photo booth had been replaced by a tattoo parlor. There were fewer carnival rides. Admission to the fair was free, but people had to pay to watch the derby. There was a line waiting to enter the stands.

I couldn't find a seat, so I stood outside the arena peering through the fence that held back the crowd. Every time a driver demolished a competitor, the spectators burst into cheers. The racetrack was illuminated by stadium lights that obliterated the stars in the sky.

On Sunday I went to the cemetery to lay flowers on my grandparents' graves. I looked for a grove of trees south of town near

Highway 71. Trees on the plains were markers of civilization, signifying the presence of a river, a town, or a burial ground.

The cemetery reminded me of Rocky Ford. Gravel roads intersected at right angles, dividing the space into rectangles. Instead of houses, there were burial plots on each block. Each one had a tombstone, flowers, and a patch of freshly mown grass. The sprinklers were running in another part of the cemetery as I knelt on the ground. I removed an artificial bouquet from a tipped-over vase and secured its base in the soil before inserting my flowers. I wondered if Uncle Phil had bought the plastic chrysanthemums. It wasn't my mother. She hadn't visited the cemetery since we left Rocky Ford.

Although Grandma Ethel had advised Mom to get an abortion, she later developed a fondness for her firstborn grandson. She spoiled me the same way she did Uncle Phil. Once she agreed to babysit when my parents went out of town. The next morning I toddled into her bedroom and crawled between the sheets. Grandma Ethel had removed her bobby pins before going to sleep and her hair hung down her back. I was surprised how much younger she looked.

When my parents returned, Mom discovered me dancing on a table in the living room. She complained to her mother, "You never let me do that!"

I mourned for Mom as I stared at my grandparents' graves. She had never had a childhood. She was forced to perform to please Grandma Ethel, but she never got to dance on the furniture.

I wandered around the cemetery reading the headstones. Next to the fence lay a slab of cement. It was surrounded by a stand of weeds that had managed to escape the gardener's scythe. The grave belonged to a two-year-old boy who had died at the turn of the previous century. The parents weren't able to afford a proper headstone. They used a stick to write their son's name, his birthday, and his date of death while the cement was wet. Embedded in the cement were some marbles arranged in the shape of a cross.

CHAPTER THREE

I Met a Traveler from an Antique Land

I spent my first week interviewing residents and attending the fair. Afterward I visited farms in the valley. They comprised a community much like Rocky Ford. Many were owned by families who were related by marriage and worked to ensure each other's success.

Like the businesses on Main Street, the agricultural industry was facing hard times. Aurora started purchasing water from the valley in the 1970s. The Denver suburb now owned the majority of shares in the Rocky Ford Ditch, one of the valley's main irrigation canals. Some farmers who had kept their water rights went bankrupt due to falling crop prices and the rising cost of fertilizer, insecticides, and heavy machinery. Others were recovering from a two-year drought and a salmonella virus that had wiped out a recent cantaloupe crop.

Farmers called Ron Aschermann a traitor when he sold his rights to Aurora. He regained their respect by working with the city to prevent the region from becoming a "Dust Bowl" now that most of the water was gone. He convinced the city to seed the valley's dry land with drought-resistant grasses to hold the soil in place. Several farmers raised cattle on acreage where they used to grow crops. Another one transformed his grassland into a nature preserve, where sportsmen hunted pheasants and quail.

In the past, said Ron, farmers flooded their fields by using metal tubes to siphon water out of the ditch. Over time they converted to drip irrigation and replaced the tubes with plastic hoses that ran underground. The holes in the "tapes" released less water and enabled farmers to irrigate their fields more efficiently.

I remembered accompanying my grandfather when he irrigated his crops. Grandpa took a two-by-four with a piece of tarp attached at one end and laid it across the banks of a ditch. He created a dam by shoveling mud on the other end of the tarp. Then he opened the ditch and let the water flow into his fields. This less sophisticated irrigation technique reminded me of the primitive farming methods practiced on the early frontier. Grandpa's father, John, was born and raised in Missouri. He married a woman from the Ozarks named Cornelia Phillips, who died when Grandpa was two. John bought a farm in Colorado in 1914 and built a dugout, where he lived with his sons. He wanted a better life for his twin daughters, Violet and Vivian, so he sent them to stay with an aunt in Lamar.

John supplemented his income by working as a field hand. He returned to the homestead occasionally to bring his sons groceries. Rupert, the eldest, recalled in an unpublished memoir how they cooked for themselves and did chores. The boys mowed hay in the summer. After letting it cure in the sun, they raked it into rows and gathered it into piles with a hay stacker. Rupert rode the horses that pulled the machine. "Vern was so small, he couldn't sit in the seat but stood up and leaned back against it. One time Gerald was riding behind me on a horse and fell into an irrigation ditch." My grandfather was four years old. "The horse was six feet high and weighed two thousand pounds."

Rupert and Vern sawed timber while Grandpa sat on the logs to keep them from rolling. Victor chopped the wood into kindling. They wrapped their feet in burlap sacks and baling wire to prevent their toes from freezing in winter. The boys hunted jackrabbits when they ran out of food and made extra money by shooting skunks and selling their pelts.

The boys hauled water from a spring located a mile from their homestead. A bull chased the boys when they approached with their buckets. The livestock destroyed their fences and ate their crops. "I think the ranchers contributed to our problems by holding their roundups next to our farm."

The only things that grew naturally on the land were "buffalo grass, cactus, and soapweeds." The ground was riddled with rattlesnake dens and prairie dog holes. The boys' subterranean dwelling was also a haven for unwelcome visitors. Once they invited a cowboy to stay in their dugout. Rupert wrote, "During the night he started shooting the rats in his bed."

John's mother came from Missouri several months every year to take care of the family. The boys strung a clothesline between the dugout and the outhouse because Grandma Sarah was blind. Otherwise, she managed without their assistance, leaving them free to play on their own. They swam in the river, picked wild grapes, and climbed trees to look for birds' nests. The boys pretended they were horses by racing on their knees with horseshoes in their hands to create tracks in the dirt.

Reading my great-uncle's memoir made me realize the

importance of family. The siblings had worked as a team. The older ones looked after the younger ones. The memoir was characterized by an absence of sentimentality. But it presented a portrait of group solidarity.

Grandpa married a Basque girl named Mary Arreguy. The Basques were also a close-knit community. They lived in the Pyrenees, seldom mixed with their neighbors, and spoke a language unknown to other Europeans. Many of them had Rh-negative blood, which made it difficult for women to reproduce when they married outside their group. Grandma miscarried several times because her body rejected the fetuses. After my father was born, she had problems getting pregnant again. She gave birth to Aunt Sherri when Dad was a teenager. Grandma hemorrhaged during delivery and almost died because the hospital didn't have a backup supply of Rh-negative blood.

My father had always wanted a sibling. He felt protective toward his sister, who suffered from ill health throughout her life. There was no rivalry between Dad and Aunt Sherri like there was between Mom and Uncle Phil. My grandparents never quarreled like my mother and father. Their home was a refuge for Cindi and me. We built forts in the hayloft, floated twigs in the ditch, played with the barn cats, and hunted in the bar pits for glass insulators that had fallen off the telephone poles. The oldest ones turned different colors with age. Cindi and I cleaned them and set them on the windowsill, where they sparkled like jewels.

When we rode in the pickup, Grandma let us guide the steering wheel. "Don't tell your mother," she said. She bought us peanuts and pop when we went to the store. I used to take a sip from my bottle, pour the peanuts inside, and watch them rise to the top. On Sunday mornings Grandma washed

Fig. 14. With my Barbie dolls on my grandparents' farm near Wiley, Colorado. Author's collection.

our hair in the sink, cradling our heads as she massaged our scalps with shampoo.

Grandpa harvested his crops in the summer. He returned at noon, scraped his boots on the doorstep, and scrubbed his hands in the mudroom with a bar of Lava soap. After lunch he took a nap, then went back to the fields. In the evening we watched *The Lawrence Welk Show* and *Petticoat Junction* while eating one of Grandma's angel food cakes.

I yearned for stability as a child. The peaceful certainty of my grandparents' marriage and the tranquil routine of farm life were preferable to the chaos I experienced at home. When

I went to Grandma and Grandpa's, I felt like I was part of a functioning family.

Unlike my grandparents, many families in the valley were destroyed by the water wars. The Knapps had settled in the region in 1908. Alden's son Jerry worked for the organization in charge of reseeding the plains. His other son, Brian, managed the farm. Brian resented Jerry for defending Aurora's stake in the irrigation canal. He stopped speaking to his brother when Jerry caught a farmer stealing water and sued on the city's behalf.

The water wars had taken a toll on the entire community. Farmers no long produced sugar beets, one of the valley's most profitable crops. The refinery once processed between fifteen and twenty million dollars' worth of sugar beets annually. It employed eighty full-time workers and several hundred part-time employees during harvest season. Many families were forced to leave town when the refinery closed in 1979.

I drove past the factory on my way to Alden's house. Its twin cement smokestacks rose above the cottonwood trees. I remembered the poem "Ozymandias" about an Egyptian pharaoh who built a statue in his image to commemorate his reign. Over the centuries it deteriorated until nothing remained but its legs.

The poem was about the vanity of human endeavor. I recalled how Rocky Ford threw a barbecue to celebrate the refinery's opening in 1909. Swink praised the factory as a symbol of the town's robust economy.

A lot had changed in the last hundred years.

Alden showed me where Kit Carson once forded the Arkansas River. The scout crossed the river on foot using the rocks as stepping-stones when he realized it wasn't deep enough to float his canoe. He commemorated his passage by naming the place Rocky Ford.

The history of my hometown reminded me of Carson's hazardous journey. Swink arrived in the valley several years after the scout, crossed the river at the same place, and built his general store. It prospered until a flood washed out the bridge at Swink's Crossing in 1921. All that remained were some concrete pilings standing in a bed of gravel. They looked like the pharaoh's statue: "Two vast and trunkless legs of stone."

I thought about Grandma Ethel as I stared at the dry riverbed. Local resident Donna Abert told me she had attended my grandmother's funeral. The preacher stood over the open grave as he pronounced the benediction, "Ashes to ashes, dust to dust." He sprinkled a handful of dirt on the coffin, and Donna heard someone mutter, "That's Ethel down to the nitty-gritty."

My grandmother lived for her children and didn't have many friends. After she died, Uncle Phil pillaged Beman Motors and Son, and Mom watched Grandma Ethel's dream dissolve into ruins.

Mom compiled scrapbooks, photo albums, and lists of achievements. They represented stepping-stones in my mother's career. The mementos were relics of an earlier era, like the rocks in the riverbed.

The last time I saw Mom, she was living alone at the ranch. Her world had shrunk to the size of a Post-it Note. Her desk was covered with little pieces of paper reminding her of things she still had to do.

Unlike my mother's scrapbooks, my great-uncle's memoir wasn't a record of personal triumphs. It was a story about a family that stuck together during difficult times. Rupert remembered one day when he and my grandfather were alone on the farm. "Dad was supposed to return with some food, but he was long overdue. The sun began to set among the clouds in the west. I told Gerald to note it well for this was Thanksgiving Day. It was a turning point in our lives. We could be thankful we were finally at the bottom. There was nowhere we could go but up."

Rupert was wrong. His father, unable to prove his claim, sold the farm and rented a place near the river called the Hard-scrabble Ranch. During the 1921 flood the family climbed onto the roof of their house, where they waited three days to be rescued. "The first day wasn't so bad. We saw our hayrack with the chickens and their nests on top go floating by, as well as the old Tom turkey, gobbling his defiance at the elements." The next day they began to get hungry. On the third day a cowboy swam to the house on horseback and removed them one at a time. They took turns sitting in the saddle while the man held the horse's tail so he wouldn't drown.

The Allmendingers left Colorado after the flood and worked as itinerant field hands until they could afford to return and buy a new farm. "Thus began our odyssey along the byways of the Central Great Plains, even as the Pioneers had done fifty years earlier."

The original homesteaders expected the valley to be a Garden of Eden. Instead, they suffered through a series of plagues like in the Old Testament. First there wasn't enough water to farm. Then there was a deluge.

I thought about the hardships my grandfather's family had endured when I interviewed Kent Lusk. His maternal great-grandparents had emigrated from Russia in 1906. Kent quit farming after the sugar beet factory closed but returned to the business when he realized it was "in his blood."

I noticed several small buildings and a Quonset hut clus-

tered together by the side of the road. A pickup filled with cantaloupes returned from the fields, and several men unloaded
the produce in the hut. They packed it in boxes as Kent came
out of the office and greeted me. He told me the farm wasn't
making much money. He hoped to keep it going so he could
pass it on to "his boys," referring to his son and a nephew
who managed the farm.

Kent showed me the new irrigation system the Knapps
had helped him install. Many farmers shared their expertise
with their friends and neighbors. Alden's daughter-in-law
was a member of the Proctor family, which owned the oldest
farm market in the valley. Gail started the Knapps's market
after marrying Brian. When the Knapps converted to drip
irrigation, they encouraged the Lusk family to do so as well.

Kent picked up a cantaloupe, carved some slices with his
pocketknife, and handed me one. He said he wanted to travel
across the country after he retired and talk with wheat farmers
in the Midwest and rice growers in Louisiana. He gestured
with his hand as if to suggest that the world was a big place
but that people had more in common than one might think.

I ate lunch at the family market, which was located on
Highway 50. It consisted of three walls and a clear plastic
sheet with a slit down the middle. The plastic kept out flies
while allowing motorists to glimpse the produce inside. Kent's
wife, Donna, was preparing food in the back room. A picnic
table held a Crock-Pot filled with beef stew, a bowl of mashed
potatoes, and a plate of homegrown cucumbers.

I sat at the table with Kent's nephew and son, a girl who
worked in the market with Donna, and a friend who came up
from Peru every summer to help harvest the crops. Customers came in the store during our meal, placed their money
on the counter, and left. Donna persuaded a visitor to join

us for lunch, and we scooted down the bench to make room for the new arrival. A fly entered the room through the open back door and swarmed among the diners gathered around the plentiful spread.

I felt a breeze and looked outdoors, where a field of purple alfalfa blossoms danced in the air.

Some of the most successful farmers in the valley were descended from Japanese immigrants. Herbert Mameda's father, Keitaro, came to the United States in 1907. He worked as a coal miner in southern Colorado, then moved to Rocky Ford and rented a farm. Keitaro started a distribution business when shippers refused to handle his produce. His eldest son died of peritonitis, and his second son, Herbert, became a dentist after World War II, so his third son took over the farm and passed it on to his sons.

I met Dr. Mameda at the family's packing shed on Highway 50. The "shed" was actually a warehouse that contained a sterilizing tank, an assembly line, and a refrigerated storage facility. A trailer heaped with cantaloupes was parked in the dock. The fruit was emptied into a tank of chlorinated water, then rolled onto a conveyor belt, where a group of women sorted the melons, removing those that were bruised or broken. Deft-fingered men packed the remaining produce into boxes, an employee stacked them on a pallet, and a forklift operator drove them away.

Everyone contributed to the family enterprise. Dr. Mameda used the profits from his dental practice to rebuild the warehouse after it had been destroyed in a fire several years earlier. The family assisted farmers whose sheds were smaller by letting them use the facility.

Farmers still employed laborers to harvest the melons. The

Fig. 15. The Mameda family's packing shed, August 2009. Courtesy Lex Nichols Photography.

fruit couldn't be picked by machines because it was too large, too fragile, and could easily break. We visited a watermelon field and watched workers toss the damaged ones aside. They left those that weren't ripe on their vines and carried the remainder to a cart hooked to a tractor.

The Mamedas owned a number of fields in the valley. Whites had refused to do business with Keitaro, but his son was now a respected member of the community, and his nephews owned one of the largest farms in the region. The Mamedas proved it was possible to achieve the American dream.

The Hispanic field hands, however, worked for minimum wage. They had fewer opportunities than other residents. The region supported the agricultural industry, but its communities were divided by economics and race.

Further tensions became apparent when I interviewed

Japanese American farmers. Some of the older ones were ambivalent about their assimilation into American society. Ugi Harada, a retired farmer in his nineties, met me at the cemetery to show me where "all the Japanese" were buried. He seemed disoriented when I arrived for our interview. "This is a pretty big cemetery for such a small town," he said as he tried to locate his brother's grave.

I asked if the grounds had once been racially segregated. But Ugi claimed the Japanese were a proud people who chose to keep to themselves. A number of them had died in the flu epidemic of 1918. Others had been killed during the Second World War. Ugi couldn't translate the inscriptions on the tombstones because he could no longer read Japanese. He had stopped speaking in his native language after his parents died. All he knew were a few simple words.

I recalled my earlier visit to the cemetery. Ugi and I both found it difficult to remember the past.

I became aware of the difference between us when visitors began pruning the shrubbery around one of the tombstones. Ugi said, "It looks like they've got a Caucasian with them."

The Issei preserved their culture by sending their children to schools where they learned their native language and the basic tenets of Buddhism. The Nissei, or second-generation Japanese Americans, discontinued the practice as they began to assimilate, but they still considered racial intermarriage taboo. Dr. Mameda told me his family ate meat "very sparingly." His mother cut it into thin slices and mixed it with vegetables. She didn't want her children to grow up like "those barbaric Americans, who ate nothing but big slabs of beef."

Dr. Mameda confided that one of his nephews had married a white woman. "Nowadays it's like marrying the girl next door," he explained with a shrug.

Japanese Americans were fully integrated into the community. But there was a new presence creating tensions among the region's inhabitants. Sumi Hiraki's father, Kentaro Takeda, had immigrated to the United States in 1914. He was broke when he arrived, so a white man purchased him a train ticket to the Arkansas Valley, where he worked for farmers until he could afford to buy his own land. Sumi married George Hiraki, the son of another immigrant. They went bankrupt during the water wars and sold their property to Diamond A, an Arizona corporation that was gobbling up the region's small family farms. Whites and Japanese Americans resented its growing presence in the valley.

The Sutos were an interracial couple who illustrated the harmonious relationship that now existed between people of different ethnicities. Peggy and Ichuro were complementary opposites. She was a gregarious woman with a boisterous sense of humor. Her husband was soft-spoken and partially deaf. I asked Ich if there were any Japanese customs his family had observed when he was a child. Peggy yelled in his ear as she translated my questions and sometimes answered on her husband's behalf. She told me they had experienced discrimination during the early years of their marriage. Children at school called their sons "fish heads." One of their sons now owned a farm in the valley. The other one, Tony, lived in Colorado Springs. He sold flowers on a street corner, dressed flamboyantly, and was active in community theater. Peggy visited Tony one day and found him at his regular spot wearing a tuxedo instead of his usual garb. He was holding a sign that read, "My mother's in town."

Tony wasn't a farmer like his brother. He wouldn't have blended in with the local community. I felt a kinship with Tony because I was a misfit as well. Dolls had been my favorite companions as a child. I escaped from the turmoil in our household by playing with Barbie in her dream house. It was preferable to the home in which I lived.

When I became an adult, Mom told me she didn't approve of my "alternative lifestyle." She predicted, "No man will ever love you as much as a woman will." I remembered how Uncle Kenny fooled around with his mistress while his wife lay on her deathbed. I recalled spending the night at my cousin's house and hearing Aunt Vicki screaming in her bedroom. I assumed she and my uncle were making love, but I later learned he was beating her. One day I went to see Dad at Beman Motors and Son. I walked in the office where Uncle Phil was kissing Louise.

I didn't want the same "lifestyle" as my parents. Marriage brought people nothing but misery.

Cindi fell in love after Mom and Dad divorced. Disillusioned by her own experience, my mother advised Cindi to have her fiancé sign a prenuptial agreement. I wondered if Mom was worried about our futures or afraid she would end up alone. She pushed us away, then made us feel there was no one we could count on but her.

My family had a history of marital discord and infidelity. The farming community was a more stable social entity, but it was also more complex than I had realized. There was no place for someone like Tony Suto. People were expected to marry, stay on the farm, and play conventional gender roles. The men worked in the fields, while their wives stayed home or tended the markets, instead of having their own careers. The valley was hostile to outsiders and had a history of racial intolerance.

During World War II the government built a Japanese internment camp in nearby Prowers County. It referred to the camp as a "pioneer community," but it was actually a prison for Americans who were believed to be in league with the enemy. Many of them were farmers and gardeners from Arizona, California, and Oregon. They planted corn, alfalfa, milo, and wheat as well as crops that had never been grown in the valley, including head lettuce, celery, and Japanese radishes.

The government allowed prisoners to help farmers during harvest season. The *Enterprise* insisted the inmates didn't pose a threat to the community. But in 1943 the paper published a cartoon entitled "Crop Saboteurs" that depicted the "Japs" as insects and showed farmers attacking them with cans of insecticide. A liquor store owner posted a sign in his window that read, "No Japs Allowed." The newspaper also printed an article dealing with rumors of a military-racial conspiracy. A boy named George Nakayama was arrested because he had allegedly predicted the exact time the Japanese would bomb Pearl Harbor. The sheriff admitted the story might have been the product of "a deceased [*sic*] mind" but warned the alternative wasn't "very pleasant to think about."

Japanese Americans who lived in the valley before the war were less likely to face questions about their loyalty. The *Rocky Ford Daily Gazette Topic* defended the residents as patriotic citizens: "Any snubs directed toward them will be resented by every fair-minded person." The next month the paper reported that four Japanese American soldiers had been treated by locals to a dinner at the Kit Carson Hotel. Two weeks later it published an article stating that Henry Harada had enlisted to fight overseas. The reporter reminded readers that the Harada family had "lived in this country for thirty-five years."

Most whites distinguished between the internees and their Japanese American friends. Local minorities had little contact with inmates during the war. I wondered if they had felt compassion for the prisoners or if they had internalized the prejudice of their white peers. I remembered a passage from my great-uncle's memoir. Rupert recalled moving to Colorado on the eve of World War I. A German syndicate owned a ranch near their homestead. "Most of their livestock were rounded up and taken away." Rupert and his brothers rustled some cattle because they considered them "community property." The Allmendingers didn't identify themselves as Germans. They were American citizens who broke the law to feed their family. They justified their actions by claiming they were fighting the "enemy."

The Allmendinger clan reminded me of the farmers I met in the valley. They worked as a unit, befriended their neighbors, and banded together against a common foe. But there was also a history of internal strife. People living in Rocky Ford in the 1960s might have assumed the Allmendingers were a typical family. They didn't know that I hid in my closet to avoid my mother's rage. As I interviewed farmers, I realized there were secrets and divisions within the community. The internment camp was disassembled after the war. No one remembered it now. The effects of the water wars were more apparent. Ron Aschermann was ostracized for selling his rights. The Knapp brothers took different sides in the feud between Rocky Ford and Aurora, while others lost their farms and their livelihoods.

Hank Konishi left California after the government confiscated his farm during World War II. He moved to the valley and worked in the orchards as a fruit tramp. He and his wife, Amy, opened a beauty salon after the war. It was next door to the liquor store that had once refused to serve Japanese American customers.

In 1986 a reporter asked Hank if he forgave the government

for having taken his land. Hank replied: "I was bitter at the time. But not anymore. That's the good thing about being young. You don't remember those things so you don't hold onto the hatred." The reporter concluded: "Hank and Amy have put their memories behind them. All they want to do is live their lives as Americans."

Hank's widow admitted to me that her husband had lied. She said he had felt "shamed and humiliated" after losing his farm. I interviewed Amy in the beauty salon and was surprised how happy she seemed, considering her husband's experience. Amy claimed she had been born with a cheerful disposition. Her name was derived from the Japanese word *amiko*, which means "laughing." Amy's father, Otomatsu, came to the United States in 1913. His wife, a picture bride named Tamiye, joined him the following year. Amy's parents worked on their farm until they died. Otomatsu passed away in his sleep at the age of eighty-seven. Several years later Tamiye was walking into Rocky Ford after hoeing onions so her daughter could "fix her hair" when she was hit by a car.

Amy had no complaints. A farmer had recently given her a watermelon. Her son-in-law, a local minister, had built a table for her bonzai trees. There was a plaque in the shop citing Amy's induction into the national Japanese American bowling league and a collection of trophies displayed on a shelf.

Amy described how she had once gone to Japan to find the village where her father was born. She felt like a tourist in a foreign country and yearned for her family back home.

All of her children had married non-Japanese. I saw a photograph of Amy posing with B. J. Thomas. It was attached to the refrigerator with a magnet that read, "We jes go together like biscuits and gravy."

Several weeks later I met Amy at a monthly luncheon

sponsored by the Japanese American Club. I arrived at the golf course restaurant, where Peggy had reserved a seat in my honor. During our meal a man named George Ashida told me his father, Eiroku, had immigrated to the valley in 1915. He irrigated his fields at night while carrying a Japanese lantern on the end of his hoe. The family couldn't afford electricity, so they put their meat in a bucket, suspended it by a rope, and lowered it into a well to keep it from spoiling. Eiroku spoke limited English. When white people spoke to him, he responded by saying, "I see." Soon people started calling him I. C. Ashida.

Another guest at the luncheon had been imprisoned in Wyoming during the war. She moved to Idaho when a sponsor agreed to let her work in his orchard. He fired her because she was too small to carry a ladder, so she hitchhiked to Colorado, where she found employment in the sugar beet fields. She laughed recalling how she would pull the beets from the ground and top off their heads with a knife. She frequently missed, cutting herself on the shin.

Amy picked up my check after lunch. I thought about the people I had met as we walked to the parking lot. Everyone had come to the valley from somewhere else. Their journeys had led them to a foreign land. Rupert recalled having arrived in Colorado late one night with his family. The train stopped at a depot on the plains. There was no one to greet them, so they hiked to Lamar carrying their suitcases. "The next morning we took a trail in a southwest direction across the unmarked prairie. The trace kept getting fainter until there was nothing left but open space."

I was raised in the valley but didn't recognize the landscape when I returned after thirty-eight years. The country was a maze of crops. The dirt roads seemed to lead nowhere. The telephone poles along the highway leaned as if they had been battered by the wind. Thunder clouds raced across the sky casting shadows on the ground. I felt like Amy did when she visited the land of her ancestors. Japan was her homeland, but it wasn't her home. Rocky Ford was my hometown, but it was no longer the place where I lived.

Amy gave me a letter when we said good-bye. She wrote that her parents had immigrated to California and put their savings in a Japanese American bank. The government seized the money after the bombing of Pearl Harbor. Amy's parents then moved to Rocky Ford, bought a farm, and rebuilt their lives from scratch. One day her father received a letter from a relative, who said her husband had died and the rest of the family was interned in a camp. She begged him to give her children a home until the war was over. Her father agreed, although "he didn't know them at the time." The Konishis were immigrants in an alien land. All they had was each other.

The letter reminded me that I wasn't alone on my journey. It was signed, "Amy Konishi (your friend)."

CHAPTER FOUR

Bad Day for a
Black Brother

In the 1960s Rocky Ford's library featured a meager selection of children's literature. The pharmacy was the only other establishment that catered to readers. A rotating stand next to the prescription counter contained an assortment of paperback books. Desperate for intellectual nourishment, I behaved like an addict when I went to the drugstore. Twirling the stand like a roulette wheel, I grabbed the first book that caught my eye when it stopped.

On my fourth attempt I hit the jackpot and selected a novel by Agatha Christie. *The Murder at the Vicarage* was set in the village of St. Mary Mead. Miss Marple, the protagonist, was a gossipy spinster who drew on her secret fund of intelligence to expose the murderers who constituted a surprisingly large percentage of the village's residents.

St. Mary Mead reminded me of Rocky Ford. It had a pub, a greengrocer's store, a tobacconist's shop, and a church surrounded by a cluster of thatched cottages. It was a peaceful rural community – the last place one would expect a serious crime to occur. I wondered as I read the novel: Who killed Colonel Protheroe, and why? Was the clock in the vicar's study altered to mislead the police about the time of the victim's death? Who was the mysterious woman whose portrait was found in the attic slashed to ribbons? And why did the Colonel's widow — who was having an affair with the handsome artist Lawrence Redding — confess to the murder when the evidence indicated she couldn't have committed the crime? Fortunately, Miss Marple was able to solve the puzzle before the murderer struck again.

I finished the novel and returned to the pharmacy to purchase other works starring Christie's incomparable sleuth. After I concluded the series, I read the adventures of Christie's other famous protagonist, the retired Belgian policeman Hercule Poirot. Unlike Miss Marple, who seldom left her cottage, her extroverted counterpart visited such exotic places as the French Riviera and Mesopotamian archaeological digs. As soon as Poirot arrived on the scene, victims started dropping like flies.

One day I was sick with the flu. I handed my mother a list of Christie novels before she went to the pharmacy to pick up my medicine. Later I awoke from a feverish sleep, noticed a book on the bedside table, and blinked at the cover. *Bad Day for a Black Brother* was written by a man named B. B. Johnson, the author of the "Superspade" series. The cover listed titles of earlier installments including *Black Is Beautiful, That's Where the Cat's At, Baby,* and *Mother of the Year.* A photograph showed the author smoking a pipe and wearing an Afro and aviator sunglasses.

The hero, Richard Spade, was a professor in the black studies department at a small university. He was also a karate expert who moonlighted as a bodyguard, protecting blacks from persecution by the "racist establishment." Spade's client in *Bad Day for a Black Brother* was a boxer who spouted self-aggrandizing poetry. He was being investigated by the government for speaking out against the Vietnam War.

Christie's characters were members of the English upper classes. Even the murderers had impeccable manners. Instead of losing their tempers and resorting to violence, they merely slipped some poison into their victims' tea. Once a killer was caught, he apologized for his actions and committed suicide, sparing taxpayers the expense of a trial.

There was no respect for the niceties in *Bad Day for a Black Brother*. Spade spent most of his time warring with "honkies." The novel introduced me to the world of racial conflict. I decided to share it with my friends when I went back to class. Mr. Toot, my sixth-grade teacher, was a recent college graduate who had been hired by the school district the previous fall. He acted as if he had been sent to Rocky Ford on a mission, like a Peace Corps volunteer assigned to work in a Third World country. During history period he strummed his guitar while the class sang folk songs by Peter, Paul, and Mary and the Kingston Trio. The songs — with their three-part harmonies and sing-along choruses — made us feel like we were sitting around a campfire roasting marshmallows instead of burning our draft cards.

I hid the book in my desk and passed it to a friend when Mr. Toot began writing on the blackboard. She held it in her lap and read the passages I had underlined. Mr. Toot turned around as she gave the book back to me. He put down his chalk, walked over to my desk, and held out his hand. The class watched as Mr. Toot opened the book and skimmed its contents. His face turned purple. "Where did you get this?" he spluttered.

Realizing he was new in town, I told him about the rotating stand at the pharmacy.

Bad Day for a Black Brother was an important chapter in my education. The only black people I knew were Bill Cosby and Diahann Carroll, TV actors who played likable, nonthreatening characters. At the time I was unaware of the race riots occurring throughout urban America. A woman from town who visited Los Angeles in 1965 wrote a letter to the *Daily Gazette* describing the Watts Riots. She sounded like a wartime reporter sending a dispatch back to the States. "First I heard a noise in the street. Then the phone went dead. You can imagine how scared I was with no man in the house." She fell asleep that night with a gun under her pillow.

Locals were frightened by reports of rioting mobs and images of a city in flames. Many of them had resided in the valley their entire lives. They might have been watching a planet explode in an alien universe.

Young people were beginning to travel abroad in the 1960s. They were eager to embrace other cultures, though they were suspicious of foreigners. High school student Mary Pat Walker wrote an article for the *Daily Gazette* about her visit to India. She described her host family as "the dearest things I've ever met." But she complained about the beggars in Bombay: "Naturally to people living like this Americans symbolize nothing but money. Their only concern is to get every cent they can. You know what a softy I've always been, but the only possible way to retain your sanity is to turn them all down." She concluded: "India is such a land of contrasts — from the beauty of the Taj Mahal to those who are more like vultures than human beings. But I like to think I'm a big enough person to find good things wherever I go."

Racial tensions increased at home as the nonwhite population continued to grow. In 1942 the United States began issuing temporary work visas to Mexican nationals, allowing them to replace American field hands who had been drafted to fight in the war. When the government terminated its contract with Mexico in 1964, residents debated whether to replace *braceros* with blacks from the South. Onion grower Vern Lofgren argued that Mexican field hands had been obligated to fulfill the terms of their contracts in exchange for their visas: "[The Negroes] can quit whenever they want. When they worked on the Western Slope picking fruit and tomatoes, they quit before the end of the season." Alden Knapp contended that "southern Negroes" were used to picking cotton and lacked "the fine finger work skills" necessary for harvesting pickles. F. X. Wathen claimed, "Negroes like hot weather, and it would be hard to get them to work in the fall." Vern L. Campbell wrote, "They're fine if they come to work but not if they come to get on welfare."

Farmers worried that blacks would be a detriment to the economy. Japanese immigrants had become prosperous landowners and respected members of the community. But some Mexican Americans who settled in the valley lacked the education and language skills necessary to secure steady employment. They had gone on welfare and become a burden to society. Farmers feared "Negroes" posed a similar threat.

Mexican Americans constituted approximately one-third of the population in Rocky Ford by the early 1960s. Roughly the same percentage of residents were welfare recipients living below the poverty line. Food stamps and Medicare became available to low-income minorities during the Johnson administration. In 1969 one woman criticized those who "choose not to work" in a letter to the *Daily Gazette*, claiming "Mexicans" used their welfare checks to buy marijuana and "stay home and make babies."

A welfare recipient responded to the accusation: "Maybe you haven't had to face the problems some of us have. That's why you see yourself fit to throw stones." Her husband had abandoned her family, and she had worked in the fields until the end of the summer but was now unemployed. "I had my Dad and relatives I could have turned to, but there was the matter of pride, and the I told you so. I know nobody owes us anything but I'm grateful for the aid we're getting."

The Head Start program offered bilingual education to Spanish-speaking children in kindergarten and elementary school. Older students who weren't served by the program became discouraged by their lack of academic progress. On October 7, 1967, a group of Mexican American teenagers became intoxicated, marched downtown, and started rioting. One resident suggested the police deputize citizens and equip them with "strong nylon ropes to catch the kids who are doing these things." People could "line the sidewalks as the guilty persons are led down the street," point "the finger of scorn," and shout "SHAME."

Minorities blamed the high school for refusing to offer bilingual courses and "Chicano" studies. On August 8, 1969, Richard Manzanares warned the system to revise its curriculum: "A minority can only be oppressed for so long. From our black brothers we have learned that we have our place in society. Hopefully we can gain it peacefully and in accordance with everyone's best civil interests. It's up to you, WASPS. Hopefully you will take heed of the pleas being made to you. Otherwise, the repercussions are too horrible to think about."

Manzanares staged a walkout at Rocky Ford High School two months later. Afterward a group of Chicano students published "a list of demands" in the *Daily Gazette*. They insisted that two Chicanos be appointed to the county school board and that bilingual classes be offered at once. They warned there would be "consequences" if the school didn't respond to their concerns.

White residents were outraged by the manifesto. Some referred to the Chicanos as "Mexicans," while others complained that reserving two seats on the school board for members of a particular ethnic group would circumvent the democratic process because board members were elected to office. The students inflamed many readers with their Marxist rhetoric, denouncing their racist "oppressors" and threatening to revolt against the "upper class."

The majority of whites had a higher standard of living than Chicanos. But they had also been struggling for generations in a region that was economically depressed. I recalled how the Allmendingers had scrimped to buy food and other necessities during World War I. Rupert wrote about how many sacks of flour his family could purchase with their government rations. Years later he still remembered that a pound of nails cost thirty-one cents. His memoir was about the cost of survival.

Mom said her parents had always been thrifty. Grandma Ethel was a bookkeeper who had married my grandfather after his second wife died. I wondered if she loved her employer or if she was looking for a chance to secure her position. My grandfather may also have been more pragmatic than I had realized. Don Gause said he threw parties and gave free tires to customers. But one of my mother's friends, Sandra Young, claimed my grandfather was "a horse trader in every sense of the word." She remembered when mom's Shetland pony gave birth to twins. My mother, who was an entrepreneur like her parents, wanted to train the ponies and sell them to the circus as a specialty act. One day my grandfather sold them to someone else because he needed the money right away. Mom came home from school and became upset when she saw a man putting them in the back of his Cadillac. She chased him down the road, and the ponies watched her until the car disappeared from sight.

Mom competed with Uncle Phil for her parents' love, but she always came in a distant second. Although my grandparents gave their son a new car every year, they claimed they couldn't buy my mother a prom dress. Grandma Ethel made her a gown out of a burlap sack. As a housewife, Mom managed the domestic accounts, a difficult task given the salary my father earned at Beman Motors and Son. One Christmas Eve Dad brought home a color TV. My mother made him return it to the store. She stretched her budget by purchasing Vienna sausages, canned vegetables, and other inexpensive foods, and she used S&H Green Stamps to pay for her kitchen appliances. The Green Stamps were the equivalent of food stamps for the middle-class poor.

My mother thought the Chicanos wanted something for nothing — special courses, government aid, and guaranteed political representation. Mom couldn't get a job and managed her family on a limited income. Minorities were in the same situation, but my mother couldn't empathize with their plight.

Donna Abert gave me a photograph of Mom posing with her classmates at Liberty Elementary School. I was surprised to see my mother surrounded by brown-skinned children with smiling faces because I didn't think she knew any "Mexicans." I remembered a white girl who had been impregnated by a Chicano and gave up the baby for adoption. One time a student stuck a wad of gum in my hair. My mother removed it with scissors, and I looked as if I had been scalped by an Indian. Afterward I vowed never to get close to a "Mexican."

Mom didn't leave Colorado until she was thirty. She had already developed her view of the world by the time she went to New York City to model. A visit to the Garment District provoked a series of anti-Semitic comments when she returned to Rocky Ford. One day she berated a salesman who bargained with her when she tried to sell some clothes to a secondhand store, claiming, "He tried to jew me down on the price."

When the Chicano students attempted to negotiate with the townspeople, Mom launched a counterattack. The next day she wrote a letter to the *Daily Gazette*. The mock manifesto, published on October 21, 1969, was entitled "'Potato Salads' Issue Demands."

Hark! — and herein find a list of demands which by all rights should be properly presented to the community of Rocky Ford at this time.

We are the German surnamed people. Hereafter we wish to be referred to as the Potato Salads. The word "German" has fallen into disrepute since Hitler started the war.

The following demands are presented on behalf of the Potato Salads:

First, we demand the respect of every non–Potato Salad in Rocky Ford. Although some members may at times digress (rob a bank, mug an old lady, spit on the sidewalk, or be picked up for indecent exposure or drunkedness [*sic*]) this shall in no way reflect itself in the attitude of the community. Potato Salads SHALL be respected.

Second, we demand that two Potato Salads be placed on the school board, three on the city council, and that every third year a German surnamed person shall be appointed mayor. It is immaterial whether these people are competent.

Third, all Potato Salad children shall be provided with a curriculum regarding their German ancestors. All such classes shall be taught by Potato Salads.

Fourth, all Potato Salad children and their adult "leaders" shall have the right to make any further demands they feel necessary to preserve their dignity. Being elected school president, cheerleader, or homecoming queen shall in no way provide adequate evidence of non-discrimination.

Fifth, all Potato Salads shall be taken off the unemployment lists. They shall be given jobs, not according to knowledge, ability or training, but because they are Potato Salads. They should preferrably [*sic*] be started out in executive positions. Why should some other race get the job just because they've worked harder for it?

If these demands are not fully met by the end of the week, we will have to seek assistance. Be advised that we have national leaders who belong to an organiztion [*sic*] called The Boiling Spuds. Their purpose is to french fry America. If they lead us well they are allowed to share hash browns over the holidays with prominent foreign officials. Some of them have even been known to smoke Havana cigars.

Most Sincerely,
Mrs. Rose Mary Allmendinger

My mother identified as a member of a group that had persecuted the Jews. I remembered the baby contest that was based on eugenics. The Germans believed in the superiority of the Aryan race. Mom wasn't an Allmendinger by birth. But she was proud of her Anglo-Saxon bloodline. She denied allegations that my grandfather traded with Indians because he was part Cherokee. Later she changed her mind when colleges implemented affirmative action. My mother told me to check the box that said "Native American." She complained about discrimination when the colleges asked for proof of my tribal affiliation.

Her editorial provoked a flurry of letters. One reader wrote: "A big hurrah for people like Rose Mary Allmendinger! We the 'silent majority' have been sitting too long in our passive, snug little world while we are being eaten alive. The Chicanos are banging a loud symbol [*sic*] in order to rally their troops. It's time for whites to fight back." A Chicano asked: "Who picked the word 'Potato Salad'? Wouldn't it be more like 'Sauerkraut with Weiners'? Except you didn't have the weiners before your ancestors came to the U.S. after doing away with the Jews."

My mother never backed down from a fight. When she and Sandra were children, they frequently rode their ponies down to the river. One day a bobcat jumped out of the bushes and chased Mom's horse across the plains. She raced back to town without a saddle, clinging to Ginger's side.

My mother liked westerns. She used to pretend she was Roy Rogers, the hero who caught the bad guys, not the pretty sidekick, Dale Evans. Mom re-created a scene from one of his movies by placing her rope in the river, hiding behind a tree, and yanking the loop when a boy entered the water and

stepped in her trap. As an adult, my mother was still playing cowboys and Indians. I reread her letter with a mixture
of pride and embarrassment. It was a knee-jerk reaction to
an editorial that raised legitimate grievances. But it was also
written by an intelligent person with a sense of humor. Her
mock manifesto reminded me of "A Modest Proposal" by
Jonathan Swift. The eighteenth-century political satirist had
proposed a solution to the Irish potato famine, suggesting the
Irish devour their young, thus ridding England of thousands
of unwanted minorities.

My mother never read "A Modest Proposal." But she had
the same misanthropic sense of humor as Swift. Although she
threatened to kill herself when she was feeling depressed, I
knew she had every intention of outliving her enemies. One
day she talked about slitting her wrists. I handed her a kitchen
knife and said, "Go ahead."

I was a lot like Mom. The best way to deal with human
misery was to treat it as a joke. Humor was a defensive weapon,
a coping device. My mother had made a statement when she
won the hat contest. Shit happened. But you could choose
to laugh about it.

My mother believed life was unfair. Chicanos needed to
accept the fact and stop complaining. She taught me that les-
son when I was child. I pretended not to care when she talked
about ending her life. It was easier to make light of her pain.

I was curious to know if race relations had improved when I
returned to Rocky Ford. I didn't know any Hispanics, the term
former Chicanos now used to refer to themselves. Most of my
neighbors where I was staying were white. Neil Van Dyk was
one of those people with whom I felt an instant connection.
He remembered my parents, and I told him I had met one of
his sons at the Rotary Club. Neil had a red brick house with

a manicured lawn. He was an upstanding citizen who owned an insurance company and was active in civic affairs.

My other neighbor was an unemployed Hispanic man who slept all day and spent his evenings drinking beer with friends. One night I was watching *The Real Housewives of Atlanta*. On TV two black housewives were chasing a white housewife down the street, trying to pull off her wig, when I heard someone start yelling next door. I saw my neighbor hop on his motorcycle, rev the engine, and peel off into the night.

Sometimes I eavesdropped on the men when they played pool in my neighbor's garage. Although they usually spoke in Spanish, the occasional repetition of the phrase "fucking Rocky Ford" indicated they were fluent in English as well.

One day I returned from an interview and noticed my neighbor sitting outside with his buddies. I decided to say hello. The men stopped talking when I approached. I told them my name and explained I was housesitting for the person next door. They gazed at me with expressionless eyes. "Well, nice meeting you," I said. I felt like a fool as I retraced my footsteps across the yard.

I understood why Hispanics were wary of whites. I also felt uncomfortable being in a town where the majority of residents were moral conservatives. I had come out to Mrs. Fox and her liberal friends, but I worried how others would react if they knew I was gay. During lunch at the farm market Kent Lusk asked if I was married. When I said no, there was an awkward silence.

I realized there were differences between my neighbor and me. I could hide my identity. His was stamped on his skin. I remembered speaking with the supervisor of the packing shed during my interview with Dr. Mameda. "You see that guy?" He pointed at an employee who had a tattoo on his arm and told me he was a gang member. "In the old days we would have run a guy like that out of town."

Some white residents were still suspicious of "Mexicans." There was a rumor that a doctor had lost his medical license after getting caught selling Vicodin on the Internet. A woman tracked down the person who started the rumor, which turned out to be false. "Never trust a Mexican," she said.

Sometimes what seemed like progress was merely an illusion. Most Hispanics in the 1960s lived north of the railroad tracks. Now the neighborhoods in the south part of town were racially integrated. The closing of the sugar beet factory had led to widespread unemployment and plummeting property values, enabling Hispanics to purchase homes that had once been out of their reach. Their upward mobility was due to Rocky Ford's economic decline.

Interracial relationships were more common today. One white woman sighed, "Who else is there to date in this town?" Others embraced the changes that had occurred over the last forty years. Larry Hollar owned the largest seed company in the valley. His son-in-law Andy Medina was expected to inherit the business. In 1969 Larry had gone to Guatemala and taught "general hygiene to people in villages." He had participated in the walkout that fall. Larry said the high school had been a crucible for whites and Chicanos in the 1960s. Most Chicano children then attended Liberty Elementary School on the north side of town. The majority of white children attended Lincoln and Washington. The races didn't mix until middle school. By the time they entered high school, the battle lines were already drawn. Now everyone attended the same school from kindergarten through twelfth grade. Larry believed integrated classrooms led to better race relations.

Some Hispanics agreed. Chris Lucero was Rocky Ford's

first Chicano police chief. Although he had retired more than a decade ago, he continued to work as a private detective, as a part-time process server, and as a court-appointed Spanish-English interpreter. I was anxious about meeting Chris as I recalled my encounter with my next-door neighbor. Chris suggested we eat at a Mexican restaurant built on the former site of my grandparents' house. As we drank cantaloupe juice, the former police chief said he remembered my mother. Chris told me he had once chased a suspect into the Beman Apartments and kicked a hole in the door. He reached through the opening, unlocked the door, and wrestled the suspect to the ground.

I remembered the apartments my mother managed after Uncle Phil left town. Most tenants couldn't afford to sign a one-year lease, so Mom let them rent by the month. As our family's financial situation got worse, she began to rent by the week. The building acquired an unsavory reputation. Someone who had known my mother said, "I'm surprised Rose Mary didn't charge by the hour."

One day Mom tried to evict a tenant who couldn't pay the rent. Cindi and I were playing in the hallway as the woman begged my mother in broken English to let her stay. A priest pleaded on the tenant's behalf, telling her the woman had two children and nowhere else to go. My mother said she also had two children. Was she supposed to let them starve so someone else's family could eat instead? Maybe the Catholic Church would like to cover the rent? The priest cursed Mom, and they continued to argue until another tenant called the police.

Chris laughed when I recounted the incident. Whites and Chicanos had more in common than they realized. Some of them had managed to improve their fortunes over time. The former chief had developed a strong work ethic as a boy living on a farm, where he picked produce and tended the stock. He was too tired to go into town at night. "When a child grows up around animals," he said, "he seldom gets into trouble."

Chris was Rocky Ford's longest-serving chief of police, a remarkable feat in a town known for racial strife. He told his wife after he was elected that he was going to treat people equally, and she replied, "In that case you're going to make everyone mad." Chris was criticized by Chicanos for using tear gas to flush out a suspect hiding in Plaza Nueva, a housing project for low-income minorities. The following year he angered a white member of the city council when he arrested the man's son for committing a misdemeanor. The father called an emergency meeting to fire the chief. He yelled at Chris during the meeting, and the chief arrested him for disturbing the peace. He ended up sharing a cell with his son.

The current chief, Frank Gallegos, also came from a modest background. His father had been a truck driver, and the rest of the family had worked in the fields to make extra money so they could buy a house on the south side of town. "I got teased for hanging out with white kids after we moved across the tracks," he said. The chief didn't have any regrets. "To this day I still have a lot of white friends."

Frank believed people from minority communities should play an active role in politics. "Hispanics like to complain about things. But when I ask them why they don't run for city council, they shrug their shoulders. A lot of them aren't registered to vote." The chief was frustrated by their lack of involvement because Hispanics outnumbered whites. "If they got organized," he said, "they'd be running this town."

Many middle-aged Hispanics I interviewed were the children of migrant field hands, lease farmers, and blue-collar laborers. They had risen into the middle class by getting an education and securing government jobs. These former Chicanos were no longer teenage radicals protesting against the establishment. They had infiltrated the system and changed it from within.

Jim Sandoval was the county commissioner. He said Hispanics "tend to accept things as they are." When he used to complain about racism in Rocky Ford, his mother would try to console him with her Catholic faith: "Don't worry. It'll be better in heaven." One day Jim replied, "I don't want it in the next life — I want it now." His high school guidance counselor had told him he "belonged in the fields," but his father encouraged Jim to apply to a nearby community college. He earned an associate degree in criminal justice and was hired by the Crowley County Correctional Institute. Jim became involved in community politics and served four years as a member of the city council, six years as the district planning commissioner, and two years as the first Hispanic mayor of Rocky Ford. Jim wasn't compensated for his service in those positions. "I just wanted to make a difference," he said. He received a full-time salary, however, as county commissioner.

Cece Zavala had also been motivated by her father to succeed. When she was a child, he tried to purchase a house on the south side of town. His agent and future neighbor told the light-skinned Mr. Zavala she was happy an Italian family was going to be living next door. When he looked confused, she realized her mistake and informed him the property was no longer available. Cece's father hired a new agent, who sold him another property a few blocks away.

Mr. Zavala had been luckier than other Chicanos because he "didn't look like a Mexican." Growing up, Cece had plenty of white friends and was the first Chicana elected head girl in high school. She studied hard because her father was a disciplinarian who advised one of her teachers to "slap her" if she didn't pay attention in class. When she considered dropping out of college, her father asked, "What are you going to do — work at the Tank 'n' Tummy?"

When I met Cece, she had been working as a social worker for twenty-three years. "With poverty comes a certain level of depression," she said. "A lot of people in this community don't go anywhere." Some Hispanics resented those among their community who tried to better themselves. She told me about an unwed teenage mother whose parents had refused to help take care of their grandchild so their daughter could go back to school. "My father used to say: 'Mexicans are like cockroaches in a jar. They all want to get out, but whenever one of them tries, the others pull it back down.'" Larry Hollar told me there were tensions in the 1960s not only between whites and Chicanos but between "lower-class Mexicans and upper-class Mexicans." The poorer members of their community resented their peers whose parents owned small businesses or had low-level government jobs.

The Hispanic people I met were successful professionals who enjoyed the respect of the non-Hispanic community. They were more fortunate than other members of their ethnic group. They had lighter complexions, had been born into middle-class families, or had been able to rise above their origins, unlike the "cockroaches" who remained in the jar. They came of age during an era of political activism and believed in the possibility of a better future. Young Hispanics were more pessimistic. They lived in a town that had been stagnating for the last forty years.

During my childhood reading enabled me to escape from my troubles at home. St. Mary Mead was different from Rocky Ford in certain respects. The murderers who lived there weren't violent or deranged. Their bloodless crimes were constructed like intellectual puzzles, and the village returned to order once the murders had been solved. Killing was an aberration in a civilized world. None of the characters resembled my mother, with her psychological reign of terror and never-ending suicide threats.

Bad Day for a Black Brother reminded me of my parents' relationship. There were differences over race and class in Rocky Ford as well. My mother belonged to a family whose name appeared on a building in the center of town. My father's relatives were farmers and sheepherders, little better than so-called Mexicans. Mom didn't associate with people of color, but Dad had some friends who spoke Spanish and knew Chris Lucero. The former chief remembered my father as "a really good guy."

Children were the biggest victims in an unhappy marriage, and young people were the ones most affected by racism. The people I interviewed were fortunate because their families had encouraged them to succeed. I thought about my neighbor who seemed to lead an aimless life and the girl who couldn't finish high school because her parents wouldn't help take care of her daughter. I remembered having been frightened when Mom fought with her tenant. The other woman had children too. I wondered if they had been listening in fear behind the apartment door.

Low-income members of minority communities now resided at Plaza Nueva instead of the Beman Apartments. I drove by the complex when I returned to Rocky Ford. Pat Sena worked for an organization that helped migrant field hands find living accommodations in the summer. She thought the city council made a mistake when it built the units on the north side of town because having them there fostered the impression that Plaza Nueva was a "tenement slum." Middle-class Hispanics referred to it as the place "where the poor people live."

The complex was located between the fairgrounds and the abandoned sugar beet factory. Tiny apartments were assembled around a neatly kept lawn. It was midafternoon, and most of the residents were working in the fields. A boy was standing in the yard hosing out a garbage can. An "Equal Opportunity" sign was posted next to the street.

I paused at the intersection, where someone had spray-painted a sign. Underneath the graffiti I read the word STOP.

CHAPTER FIVE

Remember Me

I attended the first high school football game of the season on September 4. One thing united the townspeople despite their differences. Residents were loyal to the Meloneers even though the team hadn't won the state championship since 1969, the same year the high school walkout occurred.

The Meloneers were demoted to the AA League in 1968. It was the best thing that could have happened to the struggling farming community. Rocky Ford was a Goliath compared to smaller towns in the league and won the southeastern conference title with a near-perfect record. Fowler's school superintendent became furious with the referee when his team had to forfeit the final game of the season because of a technical foul. He ran on the field and hit the man on the back. (The principal, who was present at the scene, described the blow as a "parting gesture.") Police escorted the official out of town when Grizzly fans chased him into the locker room and broke down the door.

The former Melon Capital of the World attempted to reclaim its former glory by beating Montrose at home in the quarterfinal. Residents drove halfway across the state to watch the team win the next game against Rifle. They purchased a full-page ad in the *Daily Gazette* before the final with Haxtun. The banner read: GOOD LUCK MELONEERS! The team triumphed 7–6.

My family attended every game that season. But there were tensions among us, just as there were among the residents of Rocky Ford. In high school my father had lettered in football, basketball, baseball, and track. Now he rooted for the quarterback, with whom he shared the same first name, Randy. I didn't like sports and huddled in the bleachers as the playoff season extended into winter, wishing I was home reading a book.

My father tried to interest me in athletics by starting a Little League team. He summoned me into the backyard one day and gave me a glove. Then he threw a ball at me, and I shielded my face with the mitt. I began working out with the team after playing "catch" with my father. Once I considered showing up late and telling Dad I got lost on the way to the park. But it was hard to lose one's bearings in a town the size of Rocky Ford. I became so nervous I developed a stomach ache. Mom put me to bed and informed Dad I wasn't able to attend practice that day. Then it occurred to me. Why give myself an ulcer when I could fake one instead?

My mother took me to the doctor when my condition failed to improve. He couldn't find anything wrong with my stomach, though in the process of giving me a physical, he discovered I was nearsighted. Dad was pleased when he heard the news. "No wonder you can't catch the ball. You can't even see it!"

Fig. 16. Dad, the coach of my Little League team, *top row left*. Uncle Phil, the assistant coach, *top row right*. My cousin Mike and I are standing in front of our fathers. Author's collection.

My father had initially assigned me to play first base but moved me to the outfield when the other parents complained. I spent most afternoons inspecting my cuticles and rearranging the bows on my shoelaces. I was glad to be out of the game.

Everything changed when I got glasses. I saw the skeptical expression on my teammates' faces and the eager look in Dad's eyes as the game began. In the fourth inning a batter hit a fly to right field. The ball grew larger as it came my way. I positioned my mitt, waiting for a chance to redeem myself.

The ball fell on my head and rolled to the ground.

My father didn't criticize my performance, though he must have been frustrated by my lack of athletic ability. My teammates teased me behind his back, and their parents groaned when I came up to bat. I was clumsy and nearsighted. I wore orthopedic shoes and a retainer that made me lisp. I was shamed into realizing I was different from other boys even before I knew I was gay.

Playing baseball was more traumatic than living with Mom. My father wanted to share his passion for sports. But he was living vicariously through his son. I told my father I wanted to quit the team, and he refused to concede defeat. "You're not a sissy," he said.

I was an excellent student but a terrible athlete. Dad couldn't relate to my interest in academics because he had grown up on a farm and had gone to a vocational school. My father promised to pay for four years of college and recommended I take out a loan if I wanted to go to graduate school. Dad paid for Harvard, but he stopped sending money to Cindi when she failed to complete her degree at the University of Colorado on time.

My sister's education became an issue during my parents' divorce. Dad said he and Cindi had an oral agreement. Mom argued the arrangement was unfair to my sister because Boulder was less expensive than Harvard. The judge agreed with my mother and forced my father to pay for a fifth year of college. Dad told my sister to come to his house and pick up her check. Then he took her picture down from the wall and threw it in the trash.

My mother got revenge on my father for leaving her. Dad retaliated by taking out his anger on Cindi. My sister was devastated when my father disowned her. "She was always Dad's favorite," said Mom. My mother acted as if she were fighting for her daughter's rights. But she was afraid of losing Cindi after the divorce and damaged Cindi's relationship with Dad by making her testify against him in court.

Mom implied my father loved me less than my sister. The comment confirmed my suspicion that I hadn't lived up to

Dad's expectations. Cindi felt insecure as well. She believed Mom loved me more than her. I thought my sister was paranoid. My mother didn't have a favorite. She used us as pawns because she had been manipulated in a similar way as a child. Mom resented the preferential treatment her brother had received. But Sandra disputed my mother's claim that Phil was the favorite. "It was Rose Mary all the way." Maybe Mom was wrong. Or perhaps my mother complained about her childhood because she wanted my sympathy.

Although I felt sorry for Dad when I embarrassed him on the baseball field, I was unable to comfort him. Mom used up all my emotional energy. I remembered the day she announced she was leaving home. Mom said she didn't know where she was going or when she was coming back. She told Cindi and me to decide whether we wanted to go with her or stay with Dad.

We went with our mother. She was our primary parent, the one constant in our lives. Mom considered her children a burden, but she needed us as much as we depended on her. She must not have wanted to be alone or else she wouldn't have given us the choice to go with her.

Dad was more resilient than Mom. He didn't talk about his feelings, so it was easy to forget that he had any. My mother accused me of deceiving her when I told her I was gay. I had let her think I was straight because I feared how she would react when she found out the truth. Mom acted like a jilted lover. She forced me to go to a therapist instead of acknowledging she was the one who needed counseling. My mother didn't accept responsibility for the way she treated her family.

Dad reacted quietly to my announcement. "I won't let this destroy me," he said. I spoke to my parents separately because they weren't really a couple. They were separate individuals, and I had to handle them differently. I anticipated that Mom would make a scene. It was better to get it over with as soon as possible. Although I knew Dad would remain calm, I was moved by his stoic response. I had saddened my father on previous occasions. He looked like he might not recover from this latest blow.

One summer Dad and I went on a rafting trip. Most passengers were couples who took walks in the evenings along the river while holding hands. I had never seen my parents show any affection toward each other. The insight left me feeling depressed. Dad had taken me on the trip because I was one of the few things holding his marriage together. My father wasn't reliving his childhood when he started a Little League team. He was investing in his son and committing to his role as a parent.

Many sons compared themselves to their fathers and felt inadequate. Mom once told me: "Dad has spent his life trying to win Grandpa's love. He never will." I was surprised because my grandfather had been loving toward me. He used to pinch my cheek and called me "Beaky." I flinched when he touched me, though I realized it was his way of showing affection. People sometimes hurt the ones they loved.

Now I regretted how I had treated my father. I wrote him a letter after the football game and told him I was visiting Rocky Ford. I mentioned I would pass through Colorado Springs on my way to Los Angeles at the end of the summer. He sent me an email several days later and suggested we meet for lunch. "I look forward to seeing you. Dad."

When I was a first-grader, I sat in the front row to read what my teacher wrote on the board. Mrs. Burton didn't know I was nearsighted. My frown convinced her I was more eager

to learn than the other children. She singled me out for attention, and I began to excel in her class.

Mom was pleased by my success. I had been instrumental
in preventing her from completing her education. Now I could
prove her sacrifice hadn't been in vain. She didn't know I
wanted my teacher's approval. It was a substitute for the love
I wasn't getting at home.

Mrs. Fox recalled the theatrical productions Greg LaVoi
staged as a child. I reminded her I had starred in a play she
directed about an elderly worm who lived in a library. The
"bookworm" ate the works on the shelves and slept in one
of the hollowed-out tomes. Mrs. Fox cast me as the granddaddy worm, and Mom designed my costume. I stood with
my arms at my sides as she placed the tube-shaped garment
over my head. She cut a hole in the fabric so my face could
stick out and glued cotton balls down the front to represent
my character's beard.

My mother guided me backstage on the day of the play. She
opened the book's binding, ushered me inside, and closed
the door. The curtain rose. I wiggled out of my dwelling and
encountered a group of young worms as they entered the
library.

OLD BOOKWORM: As I live and breathe, these are creatures
   of my own kind! Welcome, friends, welcome! (*No answer*)
   What's the matter? I'm a bookworm, just like you.
ALL (*looking at each other in dismay*): We're lost! The place
   is already inhabited.
FIRST BOOKWORM: We were driven from our home and a spi-
   der told us about this library. We wanted to form a colony
   and send for our families. Now we have no place to go.
SECOND BOOKWORM: And we're so hungry!

OLD BOOKWORM: But I'm the only inhabitant! There's plenty of room for you.

ALL: Hooray!

THIRD BOOKWORM: Why do you live here all alone?

OLD BOOKWORM: I don't know. I grew up here and can't remember any other life. There's a rumor I was kidnapped when I was a baby by a gypsy moth.

ALL: How sad!

OLD BOOKWORM: I've been very lonely. True — the crickets and centipedes have been kind to me, but I've always wanted friends of my own. That's why I'm so happy to have you here. There's nothing I would rather see than a community of bookworms on this shelf.

ALL (*shaking his hand one by one*): Then we are happy too!

My character was a grandfather without a family. I identified with him because reading was a solitary activity. I was the kid who didn't have any friends, the one who got picked on at recess. I was pleased with my performance and wore my costume outside after the play. A boy who was kicking a ball pointed his finger and laughed.

My teachers were my only friends until I entered fifth grade. Mrs. Verda Nolen wasn't fond of her students. Her bosom jutted out from her body like a rampart designed to keep people at bay. When I glanced up at Mrs. Nolen, I felt like a hobo living under a bridge. The world was a dark and desolate place.

Mrs. Nolen snapped at children when they asked questions and wouldn't let them go to the bathroom. Once Matt chatted with a girl during class. Mrs. Nolen twisted his ear. "Are you my friend?" she hissed. Matt whispered yes and started crying.

Mrs. Nolen loved rocks more than human beings. The *Daily Gazette* published an article about her when she converted her garage into the Museum of Paleontology. The paper announced admission was free. Mrs. Nolen planned to give away an agate necklace on opening day to boost attendance. A photograph showed my teacher standing next to a row of igneous rocks.

Mrs. Nolen made us clasp our hands behind our backs when we visited the museum so we couldn't steal her prized possessions. She instructed us to write an essay about our trip when we returned to class. I tried to ingratiate myself with Mrs. Nolen by penning a four-star review. She must have realized it was good publicity for her museum because she forwarded it to the *Daily Gazette*.

Mom was easier than my other relationships in one regard. I didn't have to pretend I liked baseball or rocks. I was a straight-A student, and she was a high school valedictorian. We understood education was important. My mother enrolled Cindi and me in one of the best schools in Colorado Springs after we moved to the ranch. She drove us to town every day and did our chores so we could study at night. Mom was thrilled when I got into Harvard because she had always wanted to go to an Ivy League school. I wouldn't have pursued a career in academia and become a professor if she hadn't encouraged me.

I was as desperate as my mother to succeed. The only way to escape from my family was to get accepted to a university on the East Coast. Harvard's acceptance letter was my ticket out of town. Nothing was going to stand in my way. I complained about having to attend Grandpa's funeral because I had an English exam. Mom looked at me in disbelief. "He was your grandfather, for God's sake!"

I was ashamed of my behavior, but I was fighting for my survival. Mom never liked my grandfather. She wasn't mad because I didn't want to go to his funeral. She knew I wanted to ace the exam to please my eleventh-grade English instructor. My mother was afraid of losing me and resented how I had become attached to my teachers. I was attracted to neurotic women like Mom. Mrs. Roberta Noland loved literature and had a cult following composed of AP students. I was her favorite disciple, the first person to raise a hand when she asked questions in class, the one who laughed the loudest at her jokes and who nodded when she made a point too subtle for my classmates to comprehend.

One year Mrs. Noland directed our high school play. She cast me as Dr. Kokintz, the scientist who invented the "Q-bomb" in the Cold War satire *The Mouse That Roared*. Mom didn't make my costume this time. My teacher and I collaborated on my "character," which consisted of an Albert Einstein wig and a thick German accent. Mrs. Noland encouraged me to ham it up in rehearsals. I was an intellectual like the granddaddy worm, but people were going to laugh at me on purpose now.

My mother wasn't happy about the hours I spent preparing with Mrs. Noland for my comic debut. She didn't say anything when I received a standing ovation after the play, but she joined me when I went to my teacher's house the following weekend for tea and cookies. My experience had taught me relationships were combative. I knew Mrs. Noland and my mother loved me because they hated each other.

The next year Mom accompanied me to high school to meet a Harvard recruiter. She bragged about my grade point average, test scores, and extracurricular activities. I recognized the look on the woman's face as she listened to my mother. "Shut up," I thought. "You're going to ruin any chance I have." I spoke to the woman again after getting accepted to

Harvard. Mom grabbed the phone from my hand. "I have a few questions," she said. I wondered if Harvard could rescind the offer. Thank goodness I had it in writing.

My mother was my biggest supporter as well as my severest critic. I realized I was still dependent on Mom when she threatened to stop paying my tuition unless I went to a therapist to "cure" my homosexuality. I did the math and told myself: "Three more years. Then I'll finally be free." But I didn't sever ties with Mom after college. Our emotional bond was too strong. My sexual orientation put a strain on our relationship, and I began to limit my visits to the ranch as she became more hostile. One Christmas she complained I was shutting her out of my life. "Maybe you should be nicer to me if you want me to come home more often," I said.

I decided to reenter therapy. The psychologist suspected Mom suffered from depression though she refused to get help. I had a choice: I could endure the abuse or end the relationship. I told the therapist I couldn't abandon my mother. He remained silent, and it finally dawned on me I couldn't save Mom. I had to create my own family by surrounding myself with people who loved me for who I was.

I remembered my mother's high school valedictory speech. "Our task is to build new roads to the future. If we lay a poor foundation, we shall find those roads filled with ruts and rough spots. Most of us will have children who need our help. We can't guide them if we have constructed our roads insecurely, so let us make our highways gleaming ribbons of accomplishment stretching ahead toward our goals."

The next morning I went to the library, where the reference room contained high school yearbooks dating back to the turn of the previous century. I read the editor's foreword in the 1956 annual: "We hope Le Cantaloupe helps you relive your high school days. May it bring you joy on a reminiscent night in the future and bind you closer to your present friends that they may not be forgotten."

I flipped through the pages until I found Mom's photograph. "Rose Mary Beman (Rosie). Valedictorian. 4 Years Pep Club. 2 Years Annual Staff. 1 Year All-State Honor Band. 2 Years Student Council. 2 Years Majorette. 2 Years Trick Twirler." My mother and a man named Byron Friedenberger had been voted the best-looking students in their class. A picture showed her pointing a pistol at Byron while he cradled a doll in his arms. Another photograph revealed her posing with classmates in front of a tree. The caption read, "Strangers in Paradise."

I wondered whether Mom was the beautiful girl named Rosie, the deranged-looking character wielding a gun, or the enigmatic figure in the final photograph.

Mom wasn't the mother I needed, but she would always be part of my life. The librarian let me borrow the annual and make copies of the pictures so I could frame them when I got back to Los Angeles.

I returned to the high school a week later to audit a history class. The flag had been lowered to half-mast in honor of 9/11. I got a visitor's pass in the front office and noticed a picture of the Meloneers mascot hanging on the wall. The watermelon had anthropomorphic facial features and stick figure limbs. It flexed its biceps and had a steroid-crazed look in its eyes.

Tammy Ridennoure greeted me before class, and I took a seat in the front row, feeling like a student again. I asked her what had inspired her to become a teacher. Tammy told me she had enjoyed reading history as a child because the books were "filled with dead people living in places I'd never get to

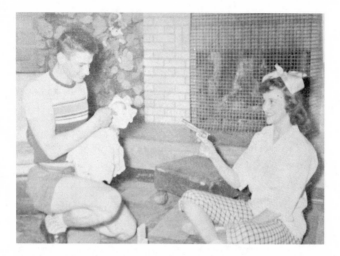

Fig. 17. A side of my mother many people didn't see, Rocky Ford, 1956. Author's collection.

go." The same was true for her students. "Hispanics tend to be family oriented. Many of them drop out of school before they graduate so they can support their families." The "pull of home" prevented them from leaving Rocky Ford to pursue better jobs.

Mom had been entangled in a similar web. She had been tied to her husband and children and forced to assume responsibility for the family's financial problems after her brother left town. I also felt the pull of home and was compelled to revisit Rocky Ford looking for insights into my mother's depression.

Tammy's students filed into class. Their current project involved researching the history of their hometown and planning a trip to the local museum. I had also been to the museum on this trip. The curator gave me a special tour because the museum had limited visiting hours. Bill Hodges showed me around the main floor, which was filled with dusty display cases. Most of the exhibits had been donated by the town's founder. I saw a photograph of Swink's original homestead, a set of plates commemorating the appearance of his watermelons at the Chicago World's Fair, and a pair of salt and pepper shakers. Bill said Swink had used bees to pollinate his alfalfa fields. The shakers were made out of beeswax.

The main floor was devoted to Rocky Ford's patriarch. The exhibits traced the story of Swink's arrival on the plains, his industry as a pioneer, and the fulfillment of his vision. The winning of the West was a source of inspiration for a town that was accustomed to defeat. Even the worms in my grade school play were colonizers seeking to establish a new society. The script offered a variation on a familiar theme and appealed to the townspeople's frontier mentality.

We went downstairs to a storage room scattered with items that weren't related to Swink. These were the pieces that didn't fit into the narrative, the discarded possessions of anonymous people, the refuse that belonged on the dung heap of history. The storage room was like my mother's hope chest. The objects had been buried rather than preserved in the basement. I had found Mom's senior yearbook in the chest and read a comment written by a fellow classmate. "Dear Rose Mary, I'll miss you but you will probably forget everyone when you get to Cornell. Bet you're glad to get out of this stinking place. At least you think you will." He sounded bitter. "You never did ride in my little Plymouth, did you? Well maybe you can when you come back from college and you're a successful businesswoman. (You!!! successful)."

Most entries began, "Best of luck in the future." Perhaps success was a matter of luck. Depression could be caused by a chemical imbalance, a bad childhood, or a series of events

Fig. 18. A local Mona Lisa, subject and date unknown. Author's collection.

that occurred later in life. Some people had the ability to cope with misfortune, and others didn't. One girl wrote, "I hope you succeed after high school. I love to watch you tap dance. It looks like it takes no effort at all." Another one added, "Write me when you're President (of what?). P.S. Always keep your swell smile."

I asked Bill if I could copy a photograph of the town's original grandstand. He took it down from the wall, and a slip of paper fell to the floor. I picked up a picture that appeared to have been taken in the 1920s. A woman dressed like a flapper sat on a bed of watermelons. A sliced piece of fruit lay at her feet. Melons had been removed from their vines and placed upright in rows behind her.

I wondered how many stories were hidden beneath the official history of Rocky Ford. Bill didn't recognize the subject. Neither of us knew how to interpret the photograph.

Tammy Ridennoure's students were considering other ways of researching their community. "Old people are a good source of information," Tammy told them. "Many of them are still coherent."

One girl asked a friend, "What does *coherent* mean?"

"It means they still remember."

Earlier I had interviewed Lyman Edgar, Tammy's father-in-law. The ninety-four-year-old farmer was regarded as Rocky Ford's unofficial historian. Lyman told me he woke up at five every morning and did stretching exercises to prevent his arthritis from spreading. After completing the chores, he ate breakfast in town and spent the rest of the morning helping his daughter Carolyn on her ranch near Timpas. He took a "siesta" in the afternoon, repeated his limbering regimen, paid bills in the evening, and went to bed around nine.

Lyman's father and uncle, Ray and Roy, used to reenact the chariot race in *Ben-Hur* every year at the fair. His aunts, Hazel and Juanita, toured in a trick riding act. Lyman was also an entertainer. Some of his tales were a little hard to believe, like the one about a mare with an acute sense of smell that helped residents locate their homes in the mud after the flood in 1921. I mentioned to an acquaintance that Lyman had told me some interesting stories. The man replied, "I'll bet he did."

Lyman had polished the shards of his memory into narrative gems. They were excerpts from the autobiography of an ordinary man.

The yearbooks in the library commemorated academic achievements, athletic victories, and other events worth recording. The earliest annual was published in 1914. A calendar listed highlights of the previous year: "October 17–18: Juniors have hayrack ride to Dye's Lake. 'Oh! The sad grey dawn of the morning after the night before.'" The calendar was a diary, an attempt to capture the memories that faded in the light of day.

Nagahar Dobashi wore a suit, a shirt with a starched collar, and a knotted cravat. His hair was parted in the middle and slicked down the sides. "*Characteristics*: Exquisitely courteous, enterprising, ambitious. *Accomplishment*: Catching the Drift of American Life. *Nickname*: George." The student had written a tribute to an extinct volcano in Japan called Mount Fuji. He described the foothills surrounded by "parks and gardens, cypresses, cherry trees, azaleas, and forests of evergreens." The lakes at its base reflected "the pure, unspotted image of Fuji on their clear crystal surfaces."

I realized George missed his home in Japan.

Other students asked to be remembered by their friends and signed their names next to their photographs. The 1934 annual belonged to Don Cline. He must not have been very popular. One comment sounded like a backhanded compliment. "Dear Donnie, Here's to a mighty swell 'guy.' Sincerely, Eileen." Another girl warned Don, "If you can't dance you can at least be careful." Most people opted for the insincere catchphrase, "I'll always remember you."

I thought about the Museum of Paleontology. It had been important to Mrs. Nolen, but to me it was just a garage with some rocks. I wondered how long the yearbooks had sat on the shelves waiting for someone to read them. Someone like me. For I was the worm who lived alone in the library.

Back then I had memorized my part by marking my lines with a pen. The ink had faded over time, and the Meloneers were no longer champions. I recalled the boy who scored the winning touchdown against Haxtun. I tried to interview him but learned he lived with his mother and "kept to himself."

Everyone in Rocky Ford knew my mother, but most people

didn't remember my father. Maybe that was better than being known as the girl who didn't go to Cornell.

I considered the strangers in my life with affection as I thought about a comment one of Don's classmates had written. "Dear Donnie, I don't really remember you. But I like you anyway."

CHAPTER SIX

A Bump in the Road

I came home after Tammy's class, and the phone rang.

"Mom died."

Cindi started crying, and another voice came on the line.

"Hi, Blake. It's Dale."

I had never met my brother-in-law. My sister had married Dale after meeting him on the Internet almost a year ago. Now Cindi was selling her house in Colorado Springs so she could move to New Mexico because Dale was a scientist at the Los Alamos lab.

"Nice to meet you," I said, trying to process my sister's news.

Dale told me a woman named Eva lived in the foreman's house and did chores for my mother. She had called 911 earlier that morning after Mom failed to answer the door. The paramedics broke into the house and found my mother slumped at her desk in the kitchen. They suspected she had had a massive heart attack. Dale said the coroner was going to perform an autopsy but it might take several days before we knew the results.

I went outside after talking to my brother-in-law. The cicadas were singing in the trees.

I wished I could mourn for my mother, but my feelings were too complex to be reduced to such a simple emotion as grief. Mom was a problem I couldn't solve. I wondered if she would haunt me for the rest of my life.

The next morning I emailed Dad, then called my sister, who sounded calmer than the day before. We discussed what to do with the body. "Just bury me in a pine box," my mother had once said, insisting nobody loved her. "Or cremate my body and flush the ashes down the toilet." My sister and I chuckled as we remembered her comment. Laughing was a way to cope with the pain.

We knew Mom wanted her ashes spread on the ranch. Cindi said it would take too long to apply for a permit, so we decided to do it illegally. No doubt our mother would have approved of our actions since she wasn't a fan of big government. "Maybe we'll get arrested!" Cindi said.

Sally told me she wanted to hold a memorial for Mom before I left Rocky Ford. I hoped it would be a cathartic experience. A friend in Los Angeles knew my mother and I had a love-hate relationship. He quipped, "You're going to have a great ending for your book now!"

It sounded like something Mom would say.

The memorial was scheduled for six o'clock the following evening in the basement of the First Christian Church. Cindi planned to come to the service with her family. She said she had reserved a room at the Edelweiss Restaurant on Friday because she wanted to hold a second memorial in Colorado

Springs. I didn't tell her I was having lunch with our father at the same place on Thursday.

My sister asked me to write our mother's obituary and contact the newspaper. I turned on my computer and stared at the screen. I had come to Rocky Ford to write a book about Mom. Now I had to reduce her life to a few biographical facts. Cindi told me not to refer to our father since their marriage was a chapter in her life Mom preferred to forget. She also recommended I leave out Uncle Phil and my cousin Mike. The edited version stated simply that Rose Mary Allmendinger was survived by her children and grandchildren.

I attached a copy of my mother's high school yearbook portrait and emailed the obituary to the Colorado Springs newspaper and the *Daily Gazette*.

"I like *survived by*," said my friend in Los Angeles.

It seemed like an appropriate phrase.

I bought a copy of the paper at the Tank 'n' Tummy the following day. Sally had added a few sentences to the obituary, indicating the memorial was also a going-away party for me. She had turned what might have been a sad affair into a communal celebration.

I met Midge Swink as she was leaving the library. "I'm sorry to hear about your mother," she said. "I didn't make the connection when you told me your last name was Allmendinger. When I saw your mother's picture, I realized, 'That's Rose Mary Beman!'" Midge recalled how Mom used to ride her horse around Rocky Ford as a child. "She looked like Elizabeth Taylor in *National Velvet*."

Bill Hodges approached me as I walked through the park and showed me an ad for Beman Motors he had discovered in an undated back issue of the *Daily Gazette*. I thanked him, and he smiled sheepishly. "Well, I better get back to work."

When I returned home, I found a pamphlet stuck in the door entitled "When Someone You Love Dies." There was a note on the cover. "Blake — This magazine will take you right to your Bible. Death is our enemy — God is the solution. Sincerely, Jennifer Nichols."

I perused the article over a cup of coffee. "It seems unfair that death should have the power to take away someone you love. The pain is not necessarily erased by being told that your loved one is in heaven. But the Scriptures indicate that it is possible to be reunited with that person right here on earth." The writer cited as evidence Christ's resurrection of Lazarus. "The raising of Lazarus is presented in the Gospel of John as a historical fact. To question its truth is to question the resurrection of Jesus himself. And to deny the resurrection of Jesus is to deny the Christian faith as a whole (I Corinthians 15:13–15)."

I tossed the pamphlet in the recycling bin.

There were almost as many churches as there were people in town. Initially, I had assumed Rocky Ford was filled with homophobic, gun-toting religious fanatics. But none of the residents talked about their beliefs during our interviews, except Jennifer Nichols. When she heard I lived in Los Angeles, she asked, "Isn't that where all the gays are?"

I answered evasively. "They're pretty much everywhere now."

During the summer I witnessed occasional outbreaks of evangelical fervor. One day I passed a billboard that read: PRAY FOR YOUR ENEMIES. YOU MADE THEM. Religious leaders posted the titles of their upcoming sermons on notice boards outside their churches. One of them boasted: I AM A

SELF-MADE MAN. "IN OTHER WORDS, YOU ARE YOUR OWN FAULT." Christianity wasn't to be taken lightly, as another sermon reminded me. JESUS IS OUR DAILY BREAD, NOT A SPECIAL OCCASION CAKE.

I felt like a sinner who had strayed from the flock as I drove to the church on the night of my mother's memorial. I wished there were more streetlamps in town as I crept down Ninth Street, stopping to read the numbers on the curb. Finally, I spotted a light shining in the basement of a building that members referred to as Fellowship Hall.

Dozens of people were milling about. Donna took me to a table featuring a guest book and a stack of sympathy cards. She had found several photographs of my mother in her freshman college yearbook, one of which showed Mom marching with the Colorado A&M band. She was dressed as a flamenco dancer in another picture. The caption read, "Rose Mary Beman tapping at International Show."

I glanced at the signatures in the guest book. The first card included a poem that had been manufactured to console the recipient. Inside another one was a ten-dollar bill.

Cindi entered the room with her family. They appeared out of place in the crowd. I started to greet them and was interrupted by a man whose picture I had seen in the beauty salon. He identified himself as the Reverend John Dell. Amy had referred to him earlier as "my Caucasian son-in-law."

The reverend suggested we form a circle and take turns introducing ourselves. My sister looked uncomfortable as a stranger reached for her hand, and I became annoyed with our host for taking control of our mother's memorial.

The circle disbanded, and he moved toward the podium. Reverend Dell began to speak about Mom, quoting from the obituary I had written.

"He didn't even know her," I thought.

Cindi wept while clutching Matt and Taylor's hands. Dale looked ill at ease. My sister had taken him to the ranch to meet his future mother-in-law several weeks earlier. Mom behaved in a courteous fashion and later emailed Dale wishing him luck in his marriage. The comment was no doubt intended sarcastically because Cindi's first marriage had ended in divorce and her ex-husband was also named Dale.

The reverend concluded his eulogy and invited my family to address the audience. I rose from my chair, wishing I had prepared a speech. Then I recognized people I had met over the course of the summer and realized —

These are my friends.

Many of them weren't acquainted with Mom. They were here tonight for my sake.

I thanked them for coming, wiped the tears from my face, and returned to my seat.

There were refreshments after the ceremony. The buffet included enchiladas, chicken lasagna, Japanese ribs, potato salad, watermelon, and homegrown tomatoes. There was lemonade, coffee, and tea as well as brownies and cake for dessert. Amy, one of the servers, gave me a hug. Peggy told me a story about when she and Ich got married. "I thought he could farm, and he thought I could cook. It turned out we were both wrong." She laughed as she scooped some food onto my plate.

Cindi and her family mingled with the guests while I chatted with a woman from Cheraw named Jean McPherson. She identified herself as a distant relative and gave me a copy of a family genealogy entitled "The Beman Family — Interesting Facts." It began with the story of John Beman and his brother William, who had come to North America from England in

1635. The Bemans had defended the colonies during the Revolutionary War, but their fortunes declined in the late nineteenth century. George and Joseph Wagoner, who were related to the Bemans by marriage, drowned while bathing in a creek in 1876. Ellen Calaher had been in the process of emigrating from Ireland when her ship hit a storm. She had been "tending her goats on deck" and was blown overboard. One entry in the genealogy was headlined "Philip Wagoner Fatally Burned." The subject had died after accidentally falling into his fireplace.

Although the history ended before Mom's father was born, Donna told me a story that gave me more insight into Grandma Ethel. "You asked me about your family, and I wasn't as truthful as I could have been. I didn't want to be judgmental," said Donna. She called Grandma Ethel a "stage mother" who had tried to push her daughter into show business. "Shirley Temple was a big star in Hollywood, so all the girls in town learned to tap dance and twirl during the Depression. Your mom was a year and a half younger and two classes ahead of her age." Grandma Ethel had entered Mom in kindergarten early to give her a head start in school. "Your mother was isolated by her age and her prominence," Donna told me. "She grew up — we thought she was just short — and she was really gorgeous. Your grandmother wanted to give Rose Mary every opportunity. Part of that could have been her living through your mom."

Grandma Ethel didn't have much of a childhood. After her parents died, she supported her four younger sisters by working as a bookkeeper. One year on her birthday the sisters thanked her for her years of sacrifice by giving her a makeover. Seating her at the vanity table, they put cosmetics on her face and styled her hair. When they finished, my grandmother stared in wonder at the beautiful stranger who appeared in the mirror.

The next day Cindi told me that the coroner had released Mom's body and that the cremation could proceed according to plan. On the death certificate, next to "Decedent's occupation," an official had written, "Entrepreneur." The cause of death was listed as "atherosclerotic cardiovascular disease." In response to the question "Interval between onset and death," the answer was, "Years."

I drove to Colorado Springs the following morning and wondered if Dad would be happy to see me. The receptionist led me to a table where an elderly man and woman were sitting. My father broke into a grin. "How . . . are . . . *you*?" he asked. He rose from his chair and extended his hand.

My father had suffered a brain aneurysm shortly after divorcing my mother. I didn't know to what extent it was responsible for his current condition and to what extent his ravaged appearance was due to the passage of time. I read between the lines on his face and searched for the man I remembered.

Dad introduced my stepmother, Dart, and the two of them expressed their condolences. I asked my father about the aneurysm that nearly took his life. When he faltered for words, Dart said, "Do you want me to tell him, Randy?"

My father nodded. Dart said they had been watching TV one night, and she asked him a question. He didn't respond, and she called an ambulance, which took him to the hospital, where he remained in a coma for several days. "The doctors advised me to stick him in a nursing home and move on with my life." Instead, she brought Dad home, supervised his physical therapy, and taught him to read and write using a children's book of ABCs. Dart had answered my email because my father couldn't write much "except for his name."

They shared the same divorce lawyer, who had introduced them to each other even though they had both vowed never to get married again. Dart was later diagnosed with multiple sclerosis. She tried to call off the wedding because she didn't want my father to spend the rest of his life nursing an invalid, but Dad refused to be dissuaded. The disease progressed slowly, allowing Dart to take care of him during his lengthy recovery.

I asked my father why he wasn't able to make his first marriage work because the obstacles he and my mother faced seemed small by comparison. Dad blamed my mother's depression. He thought Mom's need for approval was due to the fact that Grandma Ethel hadn't given her enough love as a child. My father became a commodities broker after we moved to the ranch. Goaded by his success, Mom purchased some rental properties and built a condominium complex in Colorado Springs. She competed with my father as if he were a rival instead of her husband.

"One day . . . I said to your . . . mother . . . 'Rose Mary . . . *stop.*'" Mom continued to quarrel with Dad and got angry when he didn't fight back. My father stayed in the marriage for his children's sake. He told my mother after we left for college, "That's it—I *quit.*" Dad let Mom have the ranch and the bulk of their other assets rather than haggle in court.

My mother never disclosed the terms of her property settlement. She portrayed herself as the abandoned ex-wife, making me think she had nothing left but the ranch and the clothes on her back. "Don't worry about me. I'll be fine," she said.

Now I realized she had been speaking the truth.

I asked my father, "Is it true you didn't want to see me when you were in the hospital?"

Dad became agitated. Dart explained: "Your mom said you wanted to visit your father. I told her the doctors had recommended waiting a few days until his health stabilized." Instead, my mother told me I wasn't welcome at the hospital.

I thought about all the times I had disappointed my father and assumed he had written me off.

Dad apologized for the way he'd reacted when he learned I was gay. He added, "You were a . . . pretty good . . . ball player!" He didn't blame Cindi and me for taking our mother's side during the divorce. Dart said, "I don't want to criticize your mother, but that woman had you brainwashed."

I told my father I regretted the choice I had made. "I know," he said. "And that means . . . *a lot* . . . to me."

"I don't want to rehash the past. All I want is your friend-ship . . . and your forgiveness."

"You *have* it." Dad reached across the table and took my hand.

I asked him one last question. "Is it true Mom almost had an abortion?"

My father's face twitched. Dart broke the silence. "No matter what she said, Blake — no matter how unhappy she was — you need to know one thing. *You were conceived in love.*"

"That's . . . *right!*" Dad said.

He walked with a limp as we left the restaurant. Dad told me he had gone outside last winter to check the mail, slipped on the ice, and broke his leg.

We talked about their coming to visit me next year in Los Angeles. I embraced my father when we said good-bye and promised to write. I wanted him to go to the mailbox one day and discover it had been worth the journey.

Fig. 19. Dad and me at the Edelweiss restaurant, September 2009.
Author's collection.

Later that afternoon Cindi and I met the attorney who was
handling our mother's estate. We couldn't believe Mom had
left us the ranch, seeing as she had threatened to disinherit
us whenever we incurred her displeasure. Once our mother
told us she was giving the ranch to the Colorado School for
the Deaf and Blind. Another time she considered bequeathing
it to an orphanage. "Good," said Cindi. "When you're dead,
we'll be orphans, so we'll still get the ranch."

The attorney asked what we wanted to do with the livestock. Mom had had a part-time business breeding quarter
horses. She had refused to sell them when she became
depressed because she claimed they gave her unconditional
love, unlike my sister and me.

We talked about shipping the oldest horses to a rendering
plant. "Which reminds me," I said. "We've decided to have
Mom cremated."

The attorney looked startled, then changed the subject. He referred to a lawsuit our mother had filed before she died. I wasn't surprised, given Mom's habit of suing her neighbors. Cindi said: "I wish I had a two-for-one coupon when I was shopping for crematoriums. I can think of a few people she would have liked to throw in the casket with her."

I laughed, and the attorney cleared his throat. "Yes, well. I'll draw up these papers and have my secretary call you tomorrow."

I told Cindi about my lunch with Dad after we left the attorney, and she gripped the steering wheel. "Do what you want. Just don't tell me about it."

"Dad didn't know Mom beat you," I said, ignoring her warning. Our father was devastated when he learned the truth. "If I had known that . . . we would have been . . . *out of there!*"

My sister had expected our father to rescue her. She had interpreted his failing to do so as proof he condoned our mother's behavior. Cindi blamed Dad for something that wasn't his fault yet forgave our mother for the horrible things she said and did. Whenever I criticized Mom, Cindi defended her, claiming she had had a difficult life and had no one to count on now that Dad was gone. Similarly, Mom had praised Grandma Ethel, even though my grandmother hadn't treated her as well as Uncle Phil.

I'll never understand people, I thought. I wondered if I was any wiser than I had been at the start of my trip.

Cindi took me to the house before our mother's memorial on Friday. The Hitch Rack Ranch had a notorious history. It had been founded in the early twentieth century by the warden of the Colorado state penitentiary. Roy Best had been known for making inmates bend over a sawhorse called "The Old Gray Mare" and whipping them with a wet leather strap.

When he was chastised for violating the penal code, Best replied, "The lash is a language prisoners understand." He was later removed from his post.

Best forced prisoners to work on his ranch in chain gangs. They built elaborate houses, livestock facilities, and other amenities according to the owner's specifications. In addition to the main house, there was a guesthouse with a shuffleboard court, a foreman's house, a bunkhouse, an icehouse, an out-house, a rodeo arena and announcer's booth, a main barn, two stud barns, a milk barn, a machine shop, a four-car garage, a gas pump, and a grainery bin that had once been used as a gas chamber at the prison. There was a pond with a pier and concession stand, where parties were held, and a wishing well with a false bottom in the front yard.

After Best died in disgrace, the ranch was bought by a fam-ily that lost its fortune through bad investments. The son, an alcoholic, sold the property at a bankruptcy sale. My parents restored the ranch to its former glory, but after the divorce it reverted to ruin.

The hinges groaned when I opened the gates. There was a sign on the fence that read: "Trespassers will be shot. Sur-vivors will be prosecuted."

Cindi navigated around the ruts in the road as we traveled up the driveway. The paint on the barns was peeling, and there were holes in the fence. A herd of horses grazed in Eva's yard. A killdeer ran alongside the car, pretending one of its wings was broken in its effort to lead predators away from its nest.

My sister said, "Mom started hoarding before she died." She hadn't realized the extent of our mother's illness until she entered the house after the paramedics took the body away. Mom was living like a miser. There were burned-out bulbs in the light fixtures. The roof had been damaged in a hailstorm, and the furnace no longer worked. Nor did the sinks, the toilets, the refrigerator, or other appliances.

My sister opened the door. "I can't do this again." She went into the yard and sat on the edge of the wishing well.

I stepped into the mudroom. On the floor lay a musty saddle blanket, an assortment of halters and bridles, an overturned grain bucket, a bootjack, an empty hummingbird feeder, several pairs of cowboy boots and galoshes, a Folger's coffee can filled with syringes that our mother had used to give the horses their medicine, and a leather glove that was missing its mate.

There were stacks of newspapers in the family room as well as piles of clothes, a box of Christmas tree ornaments, and unwrapped presents with the receipts attached to them. Pictures of our father had been removed from the room. A series of light-colored rectangles contrasted with the paint on the walls, which had aged over time and smelled of cigarette smoke.

My mother's office was buried beneath a mound of bulging folders, tattered phone books, and legal pads. The ashtray was filled with cigarette butts.

This was where she had died.

A path was cleared through the refuse connecting the kitchen to the rest of the house. There were rumpled sheets on my mother's canopy bed. The mattress sagged in the middle. Cobwebs hung from the bathroom ceiling, and mouse droppings littered the floor. The closet was crammed with garment bags containing outfits my mother had worn during her modeling days. There was also a shapeless nightgown, some men's extra-large T-shirts, and a pair of relaxed-fit jeans.

The toilet was splattered with feces. One of the sinks

hadn't been used since my parents' divorce. The other one was surrounded by a pair of eyelash curlers, a mascara wand, and crumpled-up tissues and cotton balls. The mirror was framed by rows of miniature lights like a makeup table in a star's dressing room.

I paused outside a door in the hallway, then peeked inside. My room looked the way I remembered it. The bed was made, and my stuffed animals rested on the pillows. There was a complete edition of Agatha Christie novels on the bookshelf and a trophy engraved with the word *Valedictorian*.

I sat on the bed and held my teddy bear. Before I left the room, I smoothed the wrinkles from the quilt, then softly closed the door.

Cindi and I went to the restaurant in the afternoon for our mother's second memorial. As I placed the guest book on the display table, I remembered how I had spent the first week of my trip attending the fair. I had spent the past week writing Mom's obituary, making plans to cremate her body, and meeting with an attorney to discuss her estate. The first memorial had been emotionally draining, but I was merely going through the motions this time. I arranged my mother's pictures on the table again and felt like a carnival barker hawking tickets to a traveling show.

After welcoming the mourners, I read emails from well-wishers who were unable to attend the memorial. Mom used to write cowboy poetry as a hobby and had hundreds of fans on the Internet. The poems were reminiscent of the satirical editorial she had published in the *Daily Gazette*. They attacked liberal politicians as well as environmentalists and urban developers who posed a threat to the ranch. Some of the muses who inspired her rants included President Bush (for), "Nobama" (against), gun control (against), and capital punishment (for).

One reader wrote, "Rose Mary had an unbelievable strength! Facing each day alone! Just her and her Animals!" He didn't mention Cindi and me. "If there is ever a book of her work published, I will be the first in line to buy one!"

Mom's persona — that of a feisty woman forced to fend for herself — appealed to western readers. Part of me wanted to tell the audience, "Here's a story about my mother you probably haven't heard before." I fantasized about getting revenge as I looked at Lois Enderud. My mother's friend had tried to convert me to Christianity by giving me a subscription to *Guideposts*, a magazine filled with inspirational articles about individuals who had overcome various forms of adversity.

I bet Mom never told Lois how she beat my sister, I thought. Then I felt ashamed as I imagined destroying Lois's faith in my mother.

Sandra told the audience that the Rocky Ford school board had objected when Grandma Ethel designed flashy outfits for the girls to wear when they twirled with the marching band. My grandmother challenged the board, which ended up letting them perform in the parade, where they caused a sensation. Grandma Ethel decided the girls should take their act to the next level by twirling with fire. She tied rags on the ends, soaked them in kerosene, and insulated the batons with asbestos. The instruments were still too hot to handle. "We threw them in the air and hoped they wouldn't come down," Sandra said.

Some guests had become acquainted with Mom after she left Rocky Ford. The Ingersolls lived on a mountaintop overlooking the ranch. My mother claimed Buck liked to spy on her with a pair of binoculars. She flipped him the bird while she was walking around her property one day. "Get a life!" she yelled.

"Rose Mary and I had our . . . disagreements," said Barbara. "But eventually I came to respect her."

The audience chuckled uneasily.

Billy Jack Barrett lightened the mood by recounting how Mom had persuaded him to breed his stud with one of her mares. She had invited him to the ranch and plied him with bourbon until Billy agreed to consider her proposal. The next night he returned, and my mother brought out the bourbon again. "I told her I'd already bred her mare after I finished the bottle. Boy, was Rose Mary pissed! 'You mean I poured all that liquor down your throat for nothing?'"

Most of the guests liked Mom in spite of her flaws. "Rose Mary taught me how to fight with makeup on," Lois's daughter Glenda recalled. She claimed my mother was a feminist role model for girls living in Rocky Ford in the 1960s. Lois said Mom's mental problems worsened after she got bucked off a horse at the ranch. She hit her head on a rock and spent several weeks in a neurological ward.

Cindi confessed the last few days had been difficult. She recounted how she had gone to the sheriff's department to get some guns that had been confiscated from our home. Our mother had rented the bunkhouse to a soldier in Iraq, who had asked her to look after the guns before he went overseas. The sheriff seized them as potential evidence, then released them after learning Mom had died of natural causes.

Cindi met a deputy as she left the department armed with an AK-47 assault rifle and other weapons. My sister and her children had lived in the foreman's house after she divorced her first husband. Our mother sometimes quarreled with

Cindi and demanded the sheriff "throw her ass off the ranch." The deputy had responded on one of those occasions.

It was an awkward moment. "They say there's such a thing as waterproof mascara. But they lie," said my sister with a catch in her voice.

My cousin Mike approached me after the service.

Uncle Phil had left Florida and moved to Colorado Springs several years earlier. He had tried to make amends with my mother, but she had no desire to renew their relationship. Mike read the obituary, in which he and his father were excluded from the list of survivors. He came to the restaurant, raised his hand when I asked if anyone wanted to speak about Mom, and I was forced to acknowledge him. "I'll never forget how Aunt Rose Mary spanked us when we misbehaved. One thing I give her credit for. She always treated me like one of the family." Cindi looked mortified as I resisted the urge to strangle my cousin.

"Excuse me," I said, turning my back on Mike. My sister and I settled the bill and headed to the ranch with her family. We considered spreading Mom's ashes next to the pond, but it had dried up due to the drought. A rowboat was tied to the pier. It lay motionless on the sun-cracked banks of the pond.

We drove to a spot where our mother had ridden before sustaining the injury that caused her to hang up her spurs. Cindi turned off the road and plunged down a culvert into an empty creek bed. The truck spun its wheels in the sand, climbed the opposite bank, and emerged in a pasture whose brittle grass was illuminated by the late-afternoon sun.

I held Mom's remains as we stood in a circle. Taylor and Matt hadn't spoken at either memorial, so Cindi asked them each to say one nice thing about their grandmother before they scattered her ashes. Taylor paused, then recalled how Mom

Fig. 20. The pasture at the Hitch Rack Ranch where my mother's ashes were spread. Author's collection.

had taught her to ride when she lived at the ranch. Matt stared at the ground after his sister finished speaking. He mumbled, "She helped me with my poetry."

Cindi lowered the tailgate so they could ride in the back. The sun set as they dangled their legs over the edge of the pickup with the ashes resting between them. The pasture was sprinkled with wildflowers and clumps of manure.

Earlier my sister had told the audience that Mom once took the children with her to do chores on the ranch. She ordered them in the back of the pickup and yelled, "Ready?" Without waiting for an answer, she stepped on the gas. Cindi ran out of the house and barely caught them in time to avert a catastrophe.

I looked over my shoulder as my niece and nephew emptied the urn and spilled my mother's remains on the ground.

Like whirling dervishes, they rose in the air.

CHAPTER SEVEN

The Diary

Cindi and I owed the Internal Revenue Service a hundred thousand dollars in inheritance taxes. We needed to clean the house, fix the heater and roof, and mend the fences before we could put the ranch on the market. In the meantime we leased the pasture and held an estate sale to pay for repairs.

There was a forest fire north of Colorado Springs in the summer of 2012. Our ranch was on the opposite side of town, but it was dry because of the ongoing drought. A neighbor stole our water, so my sister and I took him to court. We sued another neighbor who refused to honor the easement that allowed us to move our cattle from the lower pasture to the section. The mounting legal fees added to our financial woes.

I couldn't wait to get rid of the ranch. I had spent years shoveling out barns, throwing hay to the stock, and rising before dawn to break the ice in the trough. Running a ranch took a lot of money. It was also time-consuming and physically grueling. Cindi and I did the chores when we came home from college, while Mom supervised our progress or sat in the house making to-do lists for the following day. She was the warden, and we were her personal chain gang.

Roy Best also patrolled the ranch while his prisoners worked. He was accompanied by two Doberman pinschers. The dogs were so loyal to their master that an undertaker had to shoot them when the warden died because they refused to relinquish his corpse. It was rumored that Best's ghost haunted our property. I didn't believe such nonsense, but I felt Mom's presence every time I entered the house. Her spirit lingered in the air.

Cindi thought Mom wanted to punish us by leaving her affairs in a mess. It took several years to remove the trash from the house. The rental properties in town were uninhabitable. I reminded my sister that our mother suffered from depression and had a propensity for hoarding. But Cindi believed there was a twisted logic to Mom's thinking. Our mother couldn't bring herself to disinherit us. Instead, she left her estate in shambles and forced us to deal with the consequences.

Cindi discovered Mom's diary while she was cleaning the house. She advised me not to read it when I returned to the ranch. "It's really dark," she said.

The forest fires were burning when I came home that summer, and the smoke made it difficult to breathe. We camped in the unfurnished house, heated our food in the microwave, and tried to fix the pump when it broke. It continued to malfunction, so we stopped taking showers and went to the bathroom outdoors.

I read my mother's diary one evening as a storm swept through the valley. A pack of coyotes howled in the distance. The journal began the night Dad left Mom, on November 8, 1982.

The hands on my watch say 12:02 a.m. I have survived the day. Overcast skies haven't helped.

My mind tells me this can be a new beginning. For brief moments I have blood-rushing seizures of euphoria.

My lifelong problem has never been my mind—it's always been my damnable heart. But life has taught me that what my heart wants can never be. The heart must have been created by the Devil—or by God to punish bad people with. Mine has always been lonesome. Maybe that's why I love animals. They don't know what a terrible person I am.

Suicidal depression. Fancy words that mean I wish I had died long ago. Once I came close. Did I live because I hadn't paid all my dues yet? It's hard to believe the mind when it tells you there is a reason you're here. Maybe it's a religious crutch to support the weak and helpless on days like today.

Yesterday he loaded the gun for me. He assumed it would be for protection. I've never shot a gun. But it's small and he says it won't kick. Guess I would need protection if I cared enough to be afraid. Sometimes I think a handy murderer would be just the ticket. Then I could die without having to decide for sure.

My mind always rescues my heart. Will it always? I don't know. With no one around to hate me, what will I have to be angry about? Anger has saved my life many many times. But I don't want to be angry. I just want the pain to quit and the love to start. Only with my babies have I felt pain turn to joy. But one can't make a whole lifetime of motherhood. Not a whole one. Only a tiny bit of the big picture. The rest hurts. Bad.

The heart wants too much, it expects too much, it wishes too much. And it hurts too much.

Maybe I can make it one day at a time. One problem at a time. One hour at a time? One moment??

... and now it's Tuesday. I still don't know if I'll make it or not. When he left I found his wedding ring on the bar. Over. Done. Please — oh Lord — don't let me hate him. I've lived 24 years with a man who never loved anyone. Maybe his daughter. Me — never. His own folks — never. Maybe his Dad. He always yearned for his Dad. It took weeks before he cried when his Dad died. That old man never gave him what he needed. His mother was a cold cold fish.

Why didn't I die years ago? Then I'd never know the pain. Anger may be my salvation. Maybe I'll be mean, nasty and ugly.

Or maybe I'll shoot my head off. Who knows? I keep crying. He doesn't care. So I must either submit or fight like hell and defeat him. I don't want to defeat him. I don't want to submit — to lie down and roll over.

Oh, God — my poor babies!! I love them so! Why did I let them get into this?

Maybe tonight I'll find the courage to die.

... Wednesday was better — today my eyes leaked a lot but I made it through the day pretty good. I went to Denver to see the attorney.

I decided not to send the 3 page letter I wrote his mother. God! is she a nasty ole bitch. Her sweet façade covers the venom and malice of the rattlesnake. But I'm proud because I didn't crawl into the gutter with her. I told the whole sordid truth. It was meant to inflict pain upon her. She deserves it. But to get one up on her and pay her back for her calculated viciousness won't soothe my wounds.

I'm not sure I can do what I have to do.

... Thursday went by. Work consumed my energies and I didn't have to confront anyone, him or myself.

But today is Friday—and no such luck. Thank God I have the gun. Maybe I'll use it. That will be my easy way out.

November 14—Sunday night 8 p.m.—full of confusion—hope—despair—loneliness—anger—frustration. I'm scared to death and brokenhearted. He hates me very much. I'm all the bad things he ever knew—today, yesterday, tomorrow. No grace notes. No exceptions. He thinks he's been ruined. He is leaving all the dreams to run away from all the disappointments. That's his solution. Maybe we have always had the same problems. But we have never had the same solutions.

What I need and keep demanding he can't give at all. I keep pushing and he keeps building walls. Love. Warmth. Closeness. A loving touch. A tender kiss. All those things are words in a book to me. He even gave up the façade 17 years ago. Surely once in 17 years I was not a terrible person. Surely once in all that time I deserved a pat on the hand. Maybe not. If I've made him the miserable, unhappy, hate-filled man he is today then I didn't deserve his affection.

I only know I didn't mean to. I still don't know what I should have done. I wonder if I will ever know—if I can ever really understand. Maybe I'm just a curse to those around me. Maybe I'll wise up one day. And maybe I'll die in ignorance. I don't know if the pain of knowing could be worse than the pain of not knowing.

I'd do anything to put my family back together. My choices now are sink or swim. No floats available. I'll try to cut him free. But I have to find a way to go forward. The only other choice is to die. To die takes more courage than to live. I'll try. But then what??

. . . Tomorrow is the last day of November 1982. I haven't written in many days because I've avoided thinking about what is happening. I've reverted to thinking only in 10 minute intervals.

One day from now everyone will be gone — his office moved — the hired help gone — only me and the animals. Sometimes I don't know if I should rejoice or die. Will my back hold up to do the work? Will the loneliness destroy me?

I hope there really is a Lord God Almighty who will forgive me and give me strength.

. . . November 30 — 50 minutes left in this month. The office is all but vacant — pictures of my babies and a few miscellaneous items.

He hung around and sucked my blood until they were both of age. Nobody can decide who gets the kids. But who gets the coffee pot? Who gets which chair? Tonight I'm not interested in the word fair. If he wants to cut and run he can do it with an empty suitcase. I hate him tonight. I want him gone forever. If a fight begins it will never end with two whole people left. We won't both survive a battle. Maybe neither of us will survive a fight.

Blake will be home Friday — then Cindi in a couple weeks — so the real aloneness will begin mid January when they go back to school. It will be really hard then. Because then I know it will be forever for sure.

There are four bullets in the gun. Tonight I would like to use all four of them on him. Not for leaving, but for ever coming into my life. He has taken so much there is little left inside me.

. . . Today is December 16. Blake came home. Cindi will be here on Sunday. Each day I have learned to hate him more. I have little if any respect for him. In 9 days the anniversary of the Christ Child's Birth will be upon us — and all I truly have in my heart is hate. It will be a time to celebrate His birth — and I wake at night and want to kill. I pray each night for forgiveness of all my many sins and that the Good Lord will Bless my children — that He will Bless and Forgive me and give me strength to go on. I will try to shelter my children and be as calm as I can.

How do I shelter them when he gets them alone and tells my precious innocent daughter that he is looking for a "long-legged blonde with big tits" — that if she really loves a black man it's sure O K — and he tells Blake he stayed married to me because he felt sorry for me — that I've always been weird — ever since he knew me. I pulled my old scrapbook to show Blake all my elected and bestowed honors before I married — to prove to him what I used to be. Why must I defend these things?

Maybe I'll go to court. Maybe I'll kill him. Maybe I'll give it all to him and then set about seeing to it he loses it all. Or maybe he'll do that all by himself. That son of an ugly bitch would not have any business if it had not been for me and my family. He says his business is his — Big joke. He believes his own image. Male ego. He really believes he can whip the world and all the loveliest of women will swoon for him. He made some remark to Blake about checking out homosexuality too. But said he still likes women. Who else but a woman would feed his ego and tote his burdens?

Women are so dumb. Every year he spends more than he makes. He blames it on the ranch.

Maybe he'll be wealthy and sought after and magnifi-cently joyous — while I rot and starve and die. But whatever happens I have to get him gone — gone for good. I have to kill the hatred within me. With God's help maybe I can. If He will only give me His blessing, strength and courage it will be OK. I'm too fat anyway. I've been too fat since I married him. I'm always fattest when I'm unhappiest. I hope someday to be skinny again.

. . . It's 2 a.m. on Christmas morning and I can't unwind and go to bed. Pure vindictive anger. Mostly at myself but it is his head I would like to blow to smithereens.

A dinnertime talk with my son revealed more to me than any discussion we've had in a long time. I see all the mistakes — no — not ALL the mistakes I'm sure — just a very few of them. My God in Heaven how I must have helped to screw him up. His father in all his self-acknowledged perfection was a wreck at raising kids. I wasn't good — but it was NOT for lack of trying.

If I'm not careful I'll end up destroying us all to get at him. I'd like to be smart enough and selfish enough to come out of this thing with what I need and not tell him until later that I'm going for the jugular vein. I would hatefully like to make him start from scratch. I'm guessing he wants the same thing. Bloody — that will describe the ending if I'm not clever.

I haven't lived my life in selfishness — anger, per-haps — but pent up anger. Never totally released except through verbal outbursts. NEVER have I gone for real blood. If I drew any it wasn't intentionally. Maybe I did wrong — but not on purpose.

Now I know that I was wrong. It may be martyr-dom—but it doesn't bring me appreciation or love. He just grew to expect it. I must not give it.

Cindi said down at the barn the other day that she had been "taught" I was dumb—so how come I knew something??!! I let her be "taught" that!! I have to change drastically and dramatically for HER benefit if not my own. I HAVE to remember who I am, what I am—and it BETTER BE GOOD AND SUCCESSFUL.

On this day that celebrates the Birth of Our Lord, Son of God, Jesus Christ I pray for salvation—I pray that I may have the strength to do whatever should be done and the intelligence to distinguish what that may be. I pray that the Lord God Almighty will cleanse my soul of anger and hatred. For He who gave His only Son at the Cross to purge our sins will know the ultimate of all sorrows and the hopelessness of this world without Him. In Heaven's name I pray.

Amen.

It was painful to read my mother's diary even though years had passed since my parents' divorce. Mom showed me the scrapbook in her hope chest to prove she wasn't a failure. I wondered if she began hoarding because it was a way to hold onto the past.

My mother was successful, but she was also unhappy. She loved her "babies" but didn't acknowledge how she mistreated them. She was a "martyr" who supported my father and got nothing in return. She threatened to kill herself but never did. The journal was filled with anger and self-pity. It was written on a legal pad, like her editorial to the *Daily Gazette*.

Mom didn't take responsibility for destroying our family.

She prayed for forgiveness, then swore to get revenge on her husband for leaving her. I thought about Cindi when my mother insisted that if she drew any blood, "it wasn't intentionally." Maybe she was sorry her actions had unintended consequences. Her "verbal outbursts" were as bad as the whippings.

The next day I met my cousin for lunch. I invited my father and stepmother in an effort to end the family feud. Dad hadn't spoken to Uncle Phil and his son since they left Rocky Ford. Cindi refused to join us because she was furious with Mike for gatecrashing our mother's memorial.

My uncle suffered from depression. He was also an alcoholic who had abused his fourth wife, Candy, and their sons, Dusty and Beau. Mike told us the bank had foreclosed on Uncle Phil's house, forcing him to live in his car. Mike gave his father money to buy food but had little contact with him otherwise. He had the same codependent relationship with my uncle that Cindi and I had with our mother.

The following week Uncle Phil shot himself in a wooded area on the south side of Colorado Springs. A hiker discovered his body and called the police.

My uncle used a gun to do what my mother contemplated in her diary. His death made me realize I had been too harsh on Mom. She was afflicted with the same mental illness as her brother but resisted the temptation to kill herself. My mother had a will to survive, a determination to defeat her opponents.

It gave her the courage to live.

My relationship with Dad and Dart blossomed after my mother died. They came to California the following spring, and I went to Colorado each summer to spend time with my family and work on the ranch. I played Mexican dominoes with my father and stepmother's friends and swam at their gym. My mother had refused to return some of my father's possessions after the divorce. I gave him his fraternity beer stein and some photographs after making copies for the scrapbook I planned to compile.

Dad wanted to take me to Wiley. I hadn't gone there in 2009 because I was working on the book about Mom. We left the day after meeting my cousin. My father steered with his left hand because his right side was partially paralyzed. Dart helped him when he needed assistance turning the wheel.

The diner in Wiley was closed, so we ate at a truck stop in Lamar. It was over a hundred degrees outside. My face was chapped and my contact lenses were dry when we got to the farm. No one was home, so I posed in the yard while Dad took my picture. Then we drove to my great-grandparents' place, where we read a historical marker that noted that the Arreguy and Erramuspe families had founded their homestead in 1901.

I enjoyed going to Wiley, but I wasn't interested in the past anymore. What I loved was spending time with my family. The trip to Rocky Ford had been a roundabout means of coming to terms with Mom and reconnecting with Dad. My mother had forced me to choose between her and my father. After the divorce she had clung to my sister and me, then pushed us away. She had jeopardized my relationship with Cindi as well. I stopped going to Colorado because I felt guilty about visiting my sister and not seeing Mom. I acted as if I owed her a perverse kind of loyalty.

My mother's death brought the rest of the family together. Cindi met Dad at the Edelweiss a year after Mom's memorial. She cried for several hours. Now the two of them were trying to mend their relationship. They talked about issues regarding the ranch. "I forgot how much we think alike," said

Cindi. She introduced him to her children but was afraid of getting hurt again.

"He asked when my birthday was."

I told her not to take it personally. "He had an aneurysm. He wants to remember, but he can't."

Dad knew I worried that depression ran in our family. He wrote a list of things to cheer me up so he wouldn't forget. "First, you're an American citizen."

My stepmother added, "Think how lucky you are."

"Second . . . ." My father raised three fingers on his good left hand. "Harvard . . . Oxford . . . UCLA."

"You've accomplished a lot. Your dad's trying to say he's proud of you."

"Third . . . ." My father paused, then spoke in a complete sentence for the first time in three years. "*You're not like your mother.*" He said Mom tore our family apart but I was the one who brought us together again.

My mother was a hoarder, and I was a writer. I preserved my memories on paper the way she did in her diary. My book was filled with sad recollections and stories about unresolved conflicts and misunderstandings with the people I loved.

I didn't want to end up like Mom. It was time to let go of the past.

Dad let me drive the car back from Wiley. Dart glanced at him in the backseat.

"Are you awake, Randy?"

He was listening to Dart and me talk and had a smile on his face.

I merged onto the highway, and my stepmother placed her hand on the wheel.

I let it rest there.